# 5.49

## BEATING THE ODDS
## OF PANCREATIC CANCER

## By Juliette A. Guidara

Cover photo by Marisa S. Cohen Photography,
www.marisascohen.com

ISBN-10:1478273593
EAN-13: 978-1478273592
Library of Congress Control Number: 2012913243
CreateSpace Independent Publishing Platform
North Charleston, South Carolina

# 5.4%

## BEATING THE ODDS
## OF PANCREATIC CANCER

*A Remarkable Story of
Love, Collaboration and Commitment*

**A stirring, inspiring account of one couple's story of surviving cancer.**

An intimate, thoughtful look at one couple's journey through pancreatic cancer and recovery. Although Frank's outcome is foretold in the book's subtitle, Guidara's moving portrayal of the agony of coping with such a deadly cancer is riveting. She writes in chatty, rapid-fire prose of an almost daily battle to stay strong. Her desperation to find and try anything that might help him, along with her willingness to lay bare her fears and hurts — even sharing that she stockpile sleeping pills just in case Frank didn't make it — gives a raw account of the emotional roller coaster that started with a cancer diagnosis.

- Kirkus

# FOREWORD/CLARION GIVES 5 STARS

**"For those who have ever been confronted by disheartening odds— medically or otherwise—this stunning and well-written work will provide guidance, comfort, and most of all, inspiration.**

When Frank Guidara was diagnosed with pancreatic cancer, the doctor put his odds of survival at 5.4 percent, even after undergoing the conventional treatments of surgery, radiation, and chemotherapy. This memoir shares a story that will resonate with anyone who has faced such a dark diagnosis and worked to beat the odds.

Written by Frank's wife, Juliette—together with a brief first-person account of Frank's Vietnam War days—the book initially details how the couple met and married and then shifts into a tale of survival when Frank receives the diagnosis of cancer just before the couple's first wedding anniversary. To augment his chances for success and lessen her own anxiety and panic attacks, Juliette puts them both on a raw-food diet and then begins investigating Tong Ren, a Chinese system of healing that is frequently used in Asia on cancer patients. Combining alternative and conventional therapies, the couple works their way through Frank's treatment and, eventually, to his clean bill of health.

Frank's journey is a mixture of medical suspense story, guidebook for other cancer patients, and memoir of a family undergoing an enormous crisis. Mostly, though, it's a valentine. Weathering the emotional storms of chronic illness can be defeating and exhausting, and although Juliette admits that she had some very difficult days, her deep love for her husband was her lifeline.

Throughout Frank's illness and subsequent rounds of treatments, the couple's connection becomes stronger and deeper, and Juliette's commitment to their relationship comes through beautifully in her descriptions, underscoring her main points about the benefits of seeking complementary therapies, staying open to medical alternatives, and holding on to hope despite the odds. Even when sharing her most difficult and fearful moments, Juliette has an admirable level of optimism. Her writing is often light and playful, with a straightforward honesty that is well suited to the medical realities of the situation.

Photos from various excursions the couple makes that are described in the book's second half demonstrate not just success with medical treatments but also the couple's propensity for enjoying what they have right now and for helping others as well. Juliette writes, "Our journey of teaching and learning will never stop. We will continue to read and keep an open mind. Adversity is a terrible thing to waste and we are dedicated to a willingness to change and adapt."

This book is dedicated to Frank, my husband and best friend.


It is dedicated to all the people who are fighting cancer, and the people who battle alongside them.


I pray that your God sends you as many angels as he sent us, and that you have the courage to walk through the doors they show you with an open mind.


There is nothing fictitious in this book. Every name, every date and every event is true.

# ACKNOWLEDGEMENTS

To Frank, the most loving and courageous husband in the world. If you hadn't been so open minded and embracing to all the strange and bizarre "stuff" I kept subjecting you to, this book could have never been written… and you might not be alive today.

To our families and friends: My mom and dad; Rita and Xavier Haas, my sister Bernie Scheidegger and her family (Andre, Manuel and Silvio), my sister Rita Kullmann and her family (Juergen, Samuel and Michaja), my step-son Will Guidara, my sister in law Joanna Adams and her husband Bob, Frank's nephew and godson Rob Adams, Frank's niece Gina Anderson and her family (Steve, Nathan and Laura), Micki Nolan, Moira Stoddard, Doug MacLean, Joanna Reardon (Comare), Roz and Andy Puleo, Ed and Gilda Gold, Patty and Dave La Roche, Bill Timpson and Gailmarie Kimmel, Blake and Sharon Clark, Harvey Allen, Manny Costa, Tom and Pat Pedulla, Tony and Donna Cortese, John and Gemma White, Joe and Barbara Parisi, Ron and Jean Plotka, Aaron and Irma Spencer, Doug and Barbara Hilts, Richard and Alice Schaeffer, Alice Elliot, Neysa and Billy Porter and Karina Huber. Thank you for your prayers, your support and your unconditional loving friendship. Thank you for your never-ending prayers.

To our Angels: Marie-Lou Kuehne-Millerick (and her hubby Paul), Tom Tam, Cecilia Hamilton (and her hubby Michael), and Gloria Fellows (and her hubby David). Without you, there wouldn't even be a book, never mind a happy ending. You are beautiful angels whom God sent into our lives at exactly the right times. You have no idea how much we love you.

To Dr. Maury McGough – without you, we would have never found out about this disease. Thank you for caring so diligently about your patients.

Thank you for taking the time to listen to me. You, first and foremost, helped save my husband's life and words cannot do justice to how grateful we are to you.

To Dr. Cristina Ferrone, the best and most skilled surgeon in the world. Thank you for being compassionate. Thank you for caring. Thank you for being a friend.

To Dr. Dave Ryan, a "somewhat" flexible and "out-of-the-box-thinking" oncologist. Thank you for working with us and respecting our choices.

# TO MY "EDITORS"

A truly heartfelt thank you goes out to my editors who have taken the time to read and comment on this book.

Will Guidara – your initial insight when I first started to write this book was of tremendous value. I think it reads much better now ☺

Dr. Cristina Ferrone, again, thank you for being so much more than just a doctor and a surgeon. Some of this medical jargon still gives me a headache! Your support of this work is of more value than you can imagine.

To Spartacus, aka Professor Bill Timpson. Thank you for being such a literary genius. Thank you for all the insightful feedback and thank you for being such a loyal, inspiring and world-changing friend!

To Richard Schaeffer, thank you for your legal advice. Isn't it just fantastic to have a powerful attorney as a friend?!

# CHAPTERS

# FOREWORD

I have wanted to write this book for a few years now, but every time I began to think about it, I'd get stuck in some painful memory, start sobbing, and put the project aside. Then one day I got a call from Ed Gold who told me that it was selfish of me not to share what we learned. Who wants to be selfish?

So it is time. Besides, I promised God that if Frank lived, I'd tell everyone about it.

## PANCREATIC CANCER

According to the National Cancer Institute: "estimated new cases and deaths from pancreatic cancer in the United States in 2012 are:

| | |
|---|---|
| New Cases: | 43,920 |
| Deaths: | 37,390 |

Survival can be calculated by different methods for different purposes. The survival statistics presented here are based on relative survival, which measures the survival of the cancer patients in comparison to the general population to estimate the effect of cancer. The overall 5-year relative survival for 2002-2008 from 18 SEER geographic areas was 5.8%. Five-year relative survival by race and sex was: 5.4% for white men; 6.0% for white women; 4.6% for black men; 5.4% for black women". (http://seer.cancer.gov/statfacts/html/pancreas.html)

Pancreatic cancer is a disease in which malignant (cancer) cells form in the tissues of the pancreas.

The pancreas is a gland about 6 inches long that is shaped like a thin pear lying on its side. The wider end of the pancreas is called the head, the middle section is called the body, and the narrow end is called the tail. The pancreas lies behind the stomach and in front of the spine."

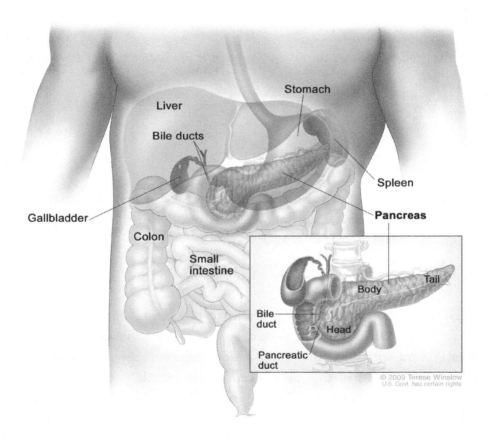

The pancreas has two main jobs in the body:

To produce juices that help digest (break down) food.

To produce hormones, such as insulin and glucagon, that help control blood sugar levels. Both of these hormones help the body use and store the energy it gets from food.

The digestive juices are produced by exocrine pancreas cells and the hormones are produced by endocrine pancreas cells. About 95% of pancreatic cancers begin in exocrine cells.

From our experience, and all the pancreatic cancer patients we talked to over the last few years, the traditional approach by the American Medical Association includes surgery (if possible), radiation (traditional or proton beam) and various forms of chemotherapy.

Realizing that following this protocol exclusively would give Frank a 5.4% five-year survival chance, we knew we had to do much more. Little did we know in the beginning what a life-changing journey we were about to undertake.

Not only did Frank sail through his big three: surgery, radiation and chemotherapy, but thanks to all the other healing modalities he was willing to put up with, he never stopped working as CEO of a substantial restaurant chain. His strength is remarkable; not only did he fight this cancer, but at the same time restructured and reorganized the company.

This is our story of beating the odds and being one of those 5.4%!

# STATEMENT

I am not a doctor, nor a licensed medical professional. I just care.

The only reason I have written this book is to enable sick people, or people caring for someone sick, to realize that they have options; if they are willing to open up to new and different ideas.

When Frank was diagnosed with pancreatic cancer and was given a 5.4% chance of survival, we were looking to our doctors for all the answers. We had no idea what other helpful, healing modalities were out there, nor did we know the facts about traditional treatment.

It's impossible for doctors to know everything. Doctors are educated to diagnose problems within the parameters of their training and prescribe various drugs that often treat symptoms. Rarely do you find one who will try to find the root cause of an ailment, then treat the cause by boosting the immune system with nutrition and / or supplements.

Luckily, Frank's doctors were and are not only dedicated professionals, but also caring people. Dr. Cristina Ferrone should set the standard of what a surgeon should be. Mass General Hospital has exceeded all of our expectations and if I ever break something, they're the first place I will go to for help.

Our hearts go out to all oncologists. Their days are filled with devastating news and death. I pray that one of these days, the pharmaceutical companies, in conjunction with the FDA, will allow oncologists and doctors to take advantage of the safe and helpful complementary modalities that are out there. Until then, their hands are tied. It seems that even suggesting an alternative treatment to the big three -surgery, chemotherapy and radiation- they could have their licenses revoked.

Despite what you're about to read, I believe that if you have cancer, and if you believe without a shadow of a doubt that traditional treatment, including chemotherapy will help you, it just might. However, if you find yourself leaning the "other way", you might want to integrate some of the alternative modalities that are available to you.

Treatment does not have to be restricted to one or the other, Western or Eastern, it can be both.

Again, I have not written this book to give advice or tell you what to do. I have simply written it to share with you what we learned, what we did, and what worked for us.

Whatever you decide, know that our thoughts and supportive prayers are with you.

# ABOUT ME

From the second I was born, I had to fight for love.

Mom and Dad were horrified to find out that they were pregnant again. After having had two girls six and five years earlier, they were comfortably "done".

As Christians, an abortion was out of the question. So to help ease their plight, they consoled themselves into believing that at least, this one would be a boy.

What a disappointment when on July 15th, 1965, I was born without a wee-wee. During her pregnancy, my Mom was so convinced that I was going to be "Konrad", she tells me that she kept referring to me as "him" for the first few weeks after I was born. I had to be the only toddler with a serious case of penis envy.

My sisters Bernie and Rita weren't thrilled, either. They had tons of fun making my life miserable. After all, a white cat was what they really wanted.

Believing early on that just being me was never going to be good enough, I tried to earn the love I so desperately craved and needed by working for it. Whatever it took, I was willing to do it, say it or show it to get it.

This need, this insecurity fueled drive to work hard to earn love probably helped save my husband's life.

I grew up in Thun, an idyllic little Swiss town on a lake, surrounded by the alps. I was skiing between my dad's legs before I could walk, and as soon as I could walk, we hiked around the mountains for days. When I couldn't walk anymore, Dad threw me on his shoulders. I was always pushed to perform physically, and tears caused by physical pain were not allowed – after all, I was Dad's tough little boy…

I was sick a lot as a kid, and even back then, accident prone. When I was one and a half, I had a brain cramp (who the hell gets those?!) and almost died. When I was six, I got driven over by a car and spent three months hung up by nails through my knees in a hospital bed. Immediately after that, I was looking at several root canals because the hospital policy did not include the brushing of one's teeth! My mom spent night after night looking after my wounds and various ailments and ridiculously high fevers, and I felt more and more like a burden.

Mom and dad were also under a tremendous amount of financial pressure at that time. My dad worked insane hours as the General Manager of a Fashion House, my mom was a piano teacher, a full time mom and waited tables at night to make ends meet. There was not a lot of time for idle cuddling.

Unconditional love came to me in the form of wet noses and fur. Every animal I saw I had to touch, hug and if at all possible, kiss. No matter how funky or old or sick, how small or big, if it had four legs and a tail, it was loved by me. Mom didn't like that very much, but dad was all for it. He never let fear enter the picture and urged me on in my quest to be "one with them". On every hike, he'd let me walk right up to any snarling, fang baring dog. I waddled over with my hand held out and without fail the dogs turned to mush. Dad hoisted me on the back of horses grazing in open fields, and once I even landed on the back of a particularly big sow.

Nature was our playground and we played every minute my parents had time off. I'm not sure if there is a mountain or a glacier in Switzerland we haven't climbed or skied on.

We shared a lot of activities, hobbies and fun as a family, but not unlike many other families, we also had issues and dramas all of which lead to my wanting to get away for a while. When I was fourteen, we all decided that I should go to Geneva for a year, working as an au pair. We found a seemingly nice family and off I went, only to be raped by the man of the house after a couple of months. My sister Bernie, who lived in Geneva at the time and with whom I'd gotten really close with, took me home. Once there, I was told to forget the whole thing. The rapist came from a very powerful family and I assume my parents were too intimidated to go after him legally. The rape would have been one thing to forget, but the cries and gut-wrenching howling of the big, beautiful Rottweiler who helplessly witnessed the whole thing – that I'll never forget.

I found another family and finished my year "abroad", fluent in French. Mom wanted me to get a job at the local post office as a government employee, but the dean of my school told them that I was too smart for that. I enrolled in a business school.

I knew I was a total misfit when I started shaving my legs and armpits after I turned sixteen. Nobody I knew did that! I rebelled against society by wearing punk clothes and black lipstick. I wanted to look, even act like a druggie, but never actually touched the stuff. I was way too scared of losing the little control I had. I assume that this period of rebellion was a direct result of the emotional scars caused by the attack in Geneva.

I worked hard for an entire summer cleaning newly built prisons to earn enough money to buy a motorcycle. I ended up in the hospital every single summer for 4 years in a row.

I had outgrown Switzerland by the time I was nineteen. Three weeks after graduating from business school I was off to America, once again as an au-pair. I had to learn English before I could get back into the business world. It was April 22$^{nd}$, 1986. The second my feet touched down on San Francisco soil and some stranger smiled at me and said hi, I knew I was home.

Three years later, I was working at Hornblower Dining Yachts in San Francisco when a friend invited me for drinks at the Pier Inn, a local joint. There I was introduced to Mr. X. I disliked him immediately and ended up in a heated argument. I told my friend and colleague Doug the next day what a jerk this guy was. But Mr. X was persistent. He was very successful and used to getting what he wanted. Over the next six months he sent drinks over whenever he saw me, all of which I sent back. One day, I was slaving away in my office, the phone rang and it was him. I was about to hang up when he brought forth his comedic genius.

Before I knew it, I was doubled over laughing. Over the next few months, he used the deceptive charms of a master manipulator and slowly I was swept off my feet while my subconscious mind was throwing one temper tantrum after another. We moved to Beverly Hills, CA and got married in 1994.

# ABOUT FRANK

---

Ah. The Italian Prince if there ever was one!

Frank had the perfect childhood. He, of course, had a wee-wee!

His mom, Virginia Daddario, was a Wellesley graduate and very intelligent. Yet, she was all mom. Her dedication and never ending attention to her children was truly amazing. Frank's dad, William Guidara, was a plasterer and from the stories I keep hearing, the most fun loving, caring dad of all time.

Frank was loved stupid from the day he was born, which was February 11, 1947. His older sister Joanna was thrilled to have a baby brother and adored him as much as his parents. She always looked out for him and their continuing loving relationship is just beautiful.

Frank grew up loving to learn and kicking butt at any sport he could get his hands on. They lived in Mattapan, a now pretty shady neighborhood of Boston, but back then it thrived with the families of returning G.I.s. All

Frank had to do was walk down his block, yelling: "Who wants to play?" and within minutes, he had a team together.

Here was an Italian boy who studied with his Jewish friends and played sports with the Irish ones. He got the best from all sides!

He went to Boston Latin School, one of the toughest in the country, and after graduating moved on to the University of Massachusetts in Amherst. After playing tackle and linebacker in high school and muscling through various injuries, he played lacrosse in college. He initially wanted to become a doctor, but changed direction and ended up in the restaurant business.

# FRANK TALKS ABOUT VIETNAM

*…but he won't tell you about his six bronze stars…*

"When I graduated from the University of Massachusetts, I immediately went to work with SkyChefs, a wholly owned subsidary of American Airlines. I felt pretty fortunate getting that job. They only hired one student from each of the restaurant/hotel programs in the country, such as Cornell, Michigan State, University of Denver. The pay was outstanding and travel back then was a true luxury and we were given free travel passes. Great pay and free travel – I felt like I was blessed.

After a brief assignment in Oklahoma City at Will Roger's Int'l. Airport, I was promoted to a bigger airport; Phoenix. This job really suited me because it required discipline and attention to detail and actually not much else. At some point, I learned about the fact that American Airlines offered a military leave of absence, which meant that seniority would accrue while you were gone. Since we were in the middle of the Vietnam war, I could only assume that I would get my draft notice and if I was able to put six months into my job with American Airlines, it would be nice to have that benefit.

So I went down to the draft board in Phoenix and asked that if they were to get my draft notice, could they hold it until I had put in my six months, which would have been in December 1968. I don't know if that was a good idea or not, because after exactly six months with SkyChefs, I got a call from the draft board to tell me that they had my draft notice. I went down to talk to them about my options. There were only two - I could either be drafted and put in two years, or I could enlist, go to officer's candidate school, and put in three years. At 21 years old, a year is a big deal. This was not just a decision about what my role would be, but about a year of my life!

After thinking about it overnight, I decided that if I were to go to Vietnam, I'd rather be the one calling the shots than having to rely on somebody else.

So I enlisted. Since I didn't have time to go home to Boston to drop everything off, I sold what little I had which was basically my Chevy Impala.

The ultimate irony was that I arrived for basic training at Fort Dix, New Jersey, on New Year's Eve, 1968. Happy New Year to me!

It was not a surprise that the following morning, G.I.'s being G.I.s, no cooks showed up in the mess hall. So there were about forty or so of us, maybe more, with nothing to eat. I'm really good with eggs! In fact, I had been practicing cracking eggs with both hands; not sure why I practiced that, but I was damn good at it. So I cooked breakfast for the guys my very first day in the army.

Lots of small memories from basic training, but probably the most meaningful is that I met my good buddy, Blake Clark – and we've been friends ever since.

Fast forward to Infantry Officer's Candidate School, Fort Benning, Georgia. I actually enjoyed my six months in OCS. I had been playing sports all my life so I was in good shape going into it. I was chosen to be president of the class and on graduation, I opted to go to Jump School, which you may know as Paratrooper Training. Heck, for six months I had looked at those jump towers and figured I might as well try them on! More opportunity to learn.

I just assumed at that point that I'd get my orders for Vietnam. I was an airborne infantry officer and they certainly were in need of those. But I was totally surprised to get orders for Fort Knox, Kentucky, to be a platoon leader for a "bunch of tanks". This was totally ridiculous but it was my opportunity to learn about engines, albeit diesel… I didn't know a thing about this stuff. How great was the Army to constantly educate me!

After serving a few months at Fort Knox, I finally got my orders for Vietnam. At Fort Knox, I had acquired a portable air conditioning unit and a reclining chair, which was <u>all</u> I owned, and the army was nice enough to send it to Boston. I knew there would be days in the jungle that I would dream about an air conditioned room.

I had some time off before I was due to report and with travel benefits from American Airlines, my parents and I went to Hawaii, where we were joined by Blake and his mother – he too had his orders for Vietnam. That was our last fling. It was during this time we made a plan to buy a sailboat (like tanks, didn't know anything about them) in New Orleans and sail thru the Panama Canal, anchor in Los Angeles and go to graduate school. This was a great plan and we kept that dream alive as we wrote to each other during our tour.

I really don't remember getting on the flight to Vietnam. I only have a memory of a conversation with a Captain who was heading back for a second tour. I didn't ask him why a second tour, I only prodded him for anything I could learn about what I was heading into.

We arrived in Long Binh in October 1970. The smells that greeted us were awful. I couldn't imagine what could cause that stench only later to find out that it was the by-product of Kerosene used to burn G.I.s' feces. Hell of an intro!

I needed to acclimate and here in Long Binh was the indoctrination center for officers. We were starving so we were directed to the mess hall, where they were serving liver, that internal processing plant – the only food I won't eat. They must have known because we had it three meals in a row. Forget about the enemy, I wasn't going to make it out of here alive…

One of the first things we were given were malaria pills. One was taken daily and one weekly. One of our tact officers had gotten malaria and I would have done anything to prevent it. When distributing the pills, they explained that some people were allergic to them. Well, I'm not allergic to anything and nothing ever bothers me. So with that confidence, I took them and that night went to have a few beers with other newly arrived officers. Actually, we had more than a few and wrapped up our first day in Vietnam crawling into our bunk beds. The memories that night are vivid. I was sleeping on a top bunk and woke up to the sounds of bombs going off. I couldn't judge their distance, nor did I know whether I could ever get used to that sound.

My stomach was really bothering me. Damn it, I might be allergic to those pills. My only solution was to get comfortable with the pain. I tried different positions to get comfortable, no success. I got out of bed and went outside to think about this problem. We were surrounded by a very high fence topped with concertina wire and there was a guard tower just to my right. I felt like I needed to take a leak. What a leak… I really had to go and when I was finally done, so were my stomach cramps. I was successful in getting past my first crisis!

It was the next day that we got our assignments. I wanted to join the 101st Airborne, the Screaming Eagles. So I tried to figure out in what order they were assigning the men, and I think it was like every fifth man who was assigned to the 101st. So I backed out of the line and once I figured out the line up, I jumped in place of the next fifth man. "Guidara – First Cav!" I didn't know much about the First Cav, but it certainly wasn't Airborne. I then remember getting on a helicopter to go join my unit, the 1st of the 7th, who at the time were on a firebase called Dragonhead in the middle of absolutely nowhere. It was the first of many helicopter rides flying over the jungle, landing on this dirt pad, with dust flying all over the place. I was brought to Col. Easterling in the headquarters tent. I didn't know what to expect. But as it turned out, the 1st Lt. who was in charge of supplies on the firebase was about to leave Vietnam. I don't remember his name but he was a good guy. Col. Easterling told me that this would now be my responsibility and to learn from the guy before he left.

At this point, I had no idea what the next hour would be like – the next morning, or that night. I had no idea what to expect about anything. I had a rifle, backpack, and a few supplies. And I had to learn how to order ammunition, food, water, etc. for the base - everything G.I.s consumed - and organize how to get supplies out to the guys in the jungle who were on patrol.

Lots of stories here about potential attacks from the NVA (North Vietnam Army) and the G.I.s coming out of the jungle, needing supplies. One of my favorite stories from Dragonhead had to do with moving the battalion to a different firebase, Cannonball.

The Colonel had a lot of confidence in me and typically a move such as this would be assigned to a captain. I might still have been a 2$^{nd}$ Lt. at that point but he wanted me to do it which meant learning all the weights of everything to be moved, such as 105 Howitzer's, lining up the number and types of helicopters needed, and making this move in as short a period as possible, since obviously we were pretty exposed once the Howitzer's and other heavy weapons were removed. If I do say so myself, I did a great job – except that after organizing everything and getting it picked up, I forgot about me. There I was after the last lift off with only my radio and my rifle. Fortunately, the colonel was still within radio range and I was able to call him to come back for me.

I knew I'd be exhausted after a couple of days going straight out and I'd made arrangements with another Lt. to save me a bunk. That night, I had a James Bond moment! Remember the James Bond movie where he was lay-ing absolutely still and cool as a cucumber while a scorpion walked across his chest? Well, it wasn't a scorpion with me; it was a gigantic rat that had lost his footing on the side of the dirt wall, next to where I was laying. All of his "ten" pounds landed smack dab in the middle of my chest! My cool imitation of James Bond lasted for exactly 100th of a second, before both rat and I went flying off the cot.

Living on a firebase was extraordinary. There was racial unrest and lots of drugs. I hadn't been exposed to either and ignored both.

It was some time later that President Nixon started bringing some troops home. The 1st Cav was part of that process. My battalion was "standing down", meaning our equipment was being sent back to the US and those of us with more time left were being reassigned.

I had been in Vietnam about five months and had seen nothing but jungle. Here we were, on the outskirts of Saigon, and I needed to see it. I forged the Colonel's name to get a jeep and talked a couple of LT's from West Point to join me. It was uncomfortable at first because we had no rifles and were fully exposed. I love learning and now I could see the famous "Saigon". The highlight was touring the American Embassy. I took pictures of course, but as we exited, the marine guards wanted the film. Photographing the Embassy was not allowed. I refused to give it up until confronted by a Marine Major at gunpoint. I gave it up and found the process interesting.

Col. Bacon had a few months prior taken over the battalion from Col. Easterling and I liked and respected him. I was still a little surprised that with all these officers in limbo awaiting new orders, I got mine first. Col. Bacon had requested me for the 2nd of the 8th, still within the 1st Cav.

I was once again helicoptered to my new firebase, Fountainhead, and reported to Colonel Bacon. He wanted me to be in charge of supplies and the firebase, like I'd always been. I can't say why because in hindsight it was pretty stupid, but I said to Colonel Bacon that I would take on that responsibility, but once I got everything organized, I wanted a platoon. I didn't want to leave Vietnam without having lived in the jungle and had combat experience.

He asked if I was trying to negotiate with him. I said "Sir, I wouldn't dare try to negotiate with you, but I want you to know how I feel." He didn't commit to anything and I went on to take charge of the firebase.

Funny story: After I got things organized, I started feeling badly for the guys out in the jungle, because all they were eating was C. Rations and L.R.R.P.'s (dehydrated meals normally given to **Long Range Recon Patrols**). Some of those C. Rations were actually left over from World War II! The L.R.R.P.'s were pretty good, but we didn't get many of them.

I would wash out some of the artillery shells from the 105s and would have a chopper ready, fill the shells with scrambled eggs and bacon, seal them, and take them out with the helicopter to the guys. I just couldn't imagine how exciting it would be for them to get hot eggs and bacon dropped at their feet, in the middle of the jungle. They deserved that extra effort, although I had no idea whether it would work. I found out later that they loved it, so I brought this process to a new level by sending out ice cream.

Sometime later, one of the companies got into a firefight, which happened now and then, but this one was different. It got extremely intense to the point where our guys were running out of ammunition, requesting more, but the chopper pilots refused to go in; it was too hot and they were taking a lot of rounds. There was one chopper pilot who had amazing balls. All I remember was his nickname "Arizona" and that he was unbelievable. So I radioed Arizona, explaining the situation and without hesitation he came out and together we loaded up the helicopter with a resupply of ammunition and took it to the guys. We typically sat on the floor of the helicopter, but in this case I sat on my steel helmet because I just couldn't imagine getting my balls shot off.

There were a lot of casualties in that firefight. The next day, we finally got the guys back to the firebase and one of the platoons which had been badly shot up refused to go back out. Colonel Bacon decided that this would be the perfect platoon for me… Needless to say, they were extremely nervous. In order to calm them down, I told them that we were going to leave the medic back at the firebase, because we wouldn't need him anymore. There was no way in hell I was going to do anything stupid and swore to keep them safe. The fact that they knew me, and knew me to be a pretty serious guy, gave them the confidence to go back out.

What a group of guys! They were from all over the country. Doug Hilts and Flash Gordon were my primary point team. Flash stayed in the military and moved around although I have not seen him. Doug still lives in upstate New York with his fabulous wife Barbara and their ever growing family. "Mississippi", (William Harrington) from Tupelo, was my radio man. "Dizzy", (Jean Blais) was only eighteen years old and got the nickname because he was a bit scattered, even though he wrote beautiful poetry. He took over for Mississippi after he went home. He lives with his wife Nancy in New Hampshire. Squad Leader Don Miller, from Yakima Washington, lives there with his wife Robin and his three kids, one married. Don was one brave guy. We had a firefight one day and we wounded this Vietcong who was in the middle of a river. After everything calmed down, all of a sudden Don jumped into the river to pull him out. However, Don forgot that he couldn't swim… He just knew he had to get this guy.

Mike Galway from Ohio is now living in St. Pete's Beach Florida with his wife Carole. Mike saved me on my first day out in the jungle when I got attacked by a colony of fire ants that had crawled down my neck, from an overhanging branch I had brushed up against. After I couldn't stand it any longer, I let out a major scream and started tearing everything off of me. Mike was on patrol right behind me and jumped right in with bug spray and saved my sorry ass. Great first impression by the new L.T.!

Kirk Davis, originally from Ohio, was also a terrific soldier. He now lives in Lake Jackson, Texas with his wife Chris.

A couple of other soldiers, who served with me in Delta Company, are also deserving of mention, such as Captain Bill Neal and L.T. Mike Martin.

As most of you know, what was different about this war was that our soldiers came and left at different times – we didn't come or leave as one unit, so there were many more men whose names I can't recall.

There were many lessons learned that I still use in life and business today. One big one is that here you are, in Vietnam, assigned a bunch of guys. Some are high school drop outs, and some used the military to get out of going to prison. Your life depends on these guys. You don't have any choice on who you get; you have to make it work for them and you. And today when I counsel young professionals, what's different is obvious – you have total choice. You can have great people work for you or not – it's your choice. Even though we had no choice in Vietnam, I was extremely lucky because regardless of their backgrounds, every single one of those guys was outstanding and a true American hero.

My superiors wanted me to stay in the military, and I actually considered it. I liked the camaraderie, I liked the discipline, and I also thought I'd like working in embassies around the world. After giving it some thought though, I realized that I wanted more than what the military could offer.

I got out of Vietnam in September of 1971, weighing 60 lbs less than when I joined the army. My shoulders and back were covered in jungle rot. I refused to take my shirt off for at least two years. I had a couple of ticks buried deeply in my feet and it took months before they came to the surface. I started smoking when I was out in the jungle, and although I planned to quit when I got out, my motivation came with the birth of my handsome son 10 years later."

# JANET AND WILL

Frank's battles continued. This time it was a long war against his wife's brain cancer. Janet developed the disease when Will was only 4 years old, and over the next 18 years Frank took care of her, never considering admitting her to a nursing home.

When asked how he held it all together, a demanding job and an even more demanding personal life, Frank simply said:

"There was a song by Kenny Rogers, about a disabled Vietnam Vet. His wife, who, because of his condition, would "take her love to town". I thought of the disabled vets that I knew and hoped that their wives took better care of them. How unfair would that be?! I believe that this song, which generated those feelings in me, carried over into the way I cared for Janet.

It all started when Janet, who was a flight attendant for American Airlines, came home from a flight and told me about a strange incident on the plane, when she dropped a light pitcher of water. We dismissed it as an accident but when something similar happened again a couple of weeks later, we knocked on our neighbor's door who was an orthopedic surgeon and asked for advice. Within two weeks, she was in surgery having been diagnosed with a tumor on her brain.

The expectation was that she would have a full recovery. Reality was very different. She never recovered any use of her left arm and lost about 50% of the use of her left leg.

We started to adjust to this handicap but as we adjusted, something else would start failing. After some years, I realized that I couldn't keep adjusting to what was occurring, and that I needed to start planning for the worst.

Will, in the meantime, was moving along in years and becoming ever more independent to the point where he was actually helping to take care of his mom.

A side story regarding Will's confidence. He was a highly energetic, fun loving, always smiling, great kid. But as time wore on and Janet became weaker, he became very introverted. So even though the housing market wasn't the best, we sold our house and moved closer to his school. This way he wouldn't have to rely on anyone to drive him to or from school. After a while, Will's personality came back. It had to be difficult for a boy his age to be so dependent on others. Now he became the center of attention because all the kids would come home with him and their parents would pick them up at "his" house.

1996 and the opportunity to take over the Wolfgang Puck Food Company in Santa Monica presented itself. So we moved. Things were going well, until Janet came down with Pneumonia for the first time. This caused her to get even weaker. The Pneumonia was followed by bed sores which had to be surgically addressed. Steadily, she got worse, to the point where I needed to find almost 24-hour help. I still took care of her at night, moving her and turning her over several times a night, to avoid getting further bed sores. One thing she never got tired of was me bringing home Wolfgang Puck's Four Cheese Raviolis!

Will was now at Cornell and our real joy was when he came to visit during holidays and summer vacation. I always encouraged Janet with events that she needed to live for, starting with Will's graduating from high school and looking forward to him graduating from college in 2001.

It became apparent that as she got weaker and with Will so far away, the opportunity to take over Au Bon Pain in Boston was something I had to do. So in January of 2000, we moved back to Boston. Once again, she got Pneumonia. This resulted in her being in a much weakened state, needing a food tube, a catheter and having oxygen pumped into her lungs via a trachea. Our only form of communication was with her blinking her eyes to my questions; once for yes, twice for no.

Will was due to graduate from Cornell the end of May, 2001. I was determined to get Janet up there for that.

As a practice run, we went to Cornell in the early Spring to watch Will play the drums at a Student Union concert. Janet's cousin Jeannie Sheppard and her husband Chooch, (a disabled Vietnam Vet) had a large RV, and they graciously took us up there. We arranged for a special medical device so that she could breathe as we brought her from the hotel to the Student Union and arranged to have a doctor on call, in case something went wrong. That's how fragile she was. Although Janet had heard Will play the drums many times in the house, she'd never actually seen him play. It was a major love fest with them grinning and smiling at each other during the entire event. We got home safely and were scheduled to leave the Saturday morning before his graduation on Sunday, May 31st.

She went into a coma on Friday, May 29th. Will drove home after graduation.  Her vital signs improved as soon as he walked into the room, and later that night, after having a bite to eat, he went back to the hospital and called me all excited that she'd come out of the coma, to see him one last time.  She made it to his graduation after all…  She passed the following morning, June 1st, 2001."

# FINALLY WE MEET

In the Fall of 1996, I got a call from a headhunter and was talked into interviewing for a position at the Wolfgang Puck Food Company in Santa Monica. The new President and CEO, Frank Guidara, was looking for an executive assistant.

I was walking down 3rd Avenue in Santa Monica, wearing a sharp, black suit with pink trim, ready for my interview with Frank at the Wolfgang Puck Express. The second I saw him, I thought *"oops, this could be trouble. The guy is way too handsome!"* I got over that and behaved like the professional that I am. I thought that the interview went really well, only to get a rejection the next day. Really?! I had never been turned down for a job I interviewed for!

A few months later, someone from Human Resources called and asked me if I was still interested and available. I said yes. After I filled out the enrollment forms, I couldn't help but ask:

"Why now? And do you know why he didn't hire me the first time?"

With a devilish grin she said:

"Juliette, don't ever, ever wear anything pink around Frank. I mean it!"

I couldn't believe it. I didn't get the job because my suit had some pink it in? No way. Later on, I came to find out that yes, Frank abhors the color pink, but it was my being Swiss that scared him off. He needed someone flexible and in his experience, the Swiss were anything but. Had he told me, I could've given him a hundred reasons why I left Switzerland – all of which had to do with the inflexibility of the Swiss!

From the first day I worked for him, I was impressed with his character and leadership qualities. Watching him over the next 3 years battling corporate and personal challenges that would knock every normal man flat on his butt, I gained a tremendous amount of respect for the guy. Here's a man who worked 7 days a week, then went home dog-tired to care for a 100% disabled wife. I thought he was joking when he told me that he took naps at red lights…

The first time I heard Frank laugh was about a year into our working together. I always thought of Frank as an "East Coast Stiff" with no sense of humor. How wrong I was… So there I was, at the bar of Obachine, Wolfgang's latest restaurant. I was surrounded by a bunch of cowork-ers and enjoyed a couple of glasses of wine. That night, we had a come-dian working the bar. Frank, Wolfgang and his wife Barbara, and a bunch of other executives were sitting at a table talking shop. The comedian announced that he was taking a break and that the microphone was avail-able to anyone during that time.

"Jules, I dare you to go up there and tell a joke," a buddy challenged.

"Are you kidding me? No way!"

"Chicken!"

"Oh come on, Jules, you rock at telling jokes. Go up there. Go!" My friends spurred me on.

"Ok fine. Let me finish my wine and I'll do it."

So there I was, on stage, microphone in hand, trying to remember the cleanest joke I knew. Then it came to me: Little Red Riding Hood! That sounded so sweet and nice and before I knew it, I had begun:

"So one day, little Red Riding Hood goes skipping down the forest when she comes to a crossroad. Out of nowhere an old wizard appeared and said: Little Red Riding Hood, you can't go down this way, the big bad wolf…."

*Oh no!!!* I just remembered that this was not a clean, sweet joke at all. Not at all! I stopped in the middle of the sentence and didn't know what to do. Everybody was staring at me, trying to figure out what I was doing. *Ok,* I said to myself, *I can either look like a total idiot and leave the stage, or I can finish the joke and get fired tomorrow.* Since I don't like looking like a total idiot, I finished the terrible joke with its rather disgraceful punch line.

The silence was deafening. Then, Frank started to roar! He was laughing his guts out until tears were running down his cheeks. He was soon joined by Wolf and the others. I wasn't going to get fired after all.

That night, I decided to make it my mission to keep Frank laughing; now that I knew he could.

Once in a while I'd walk into his office and tell him something funny. He was always receptive to a good laugh and I kept them coming. We had another two great years of working together, sharing mutual respect for one another. And no, we never had anything romantic going on (except once, in my dream).

Janet was getting worse and Frank decided to move back to Boston, where she felt more at home. He took over Au Bon Pain as CEO while I stayed in LA and began climbing the corporate ladder.

Every few months I sent Frank some funnies via mail or email to keep him laughing (that was, after all, my responsibility).

> **COURAGE DOES NOT ALWAYS ROAR. SOMETIMES IT IS A QUIET VOICE AT THE END OF THE DAY SAYING…. "I WILL TRY AGAIN TOMORROW."**
>
> **Mary Anne Radmacher**

# ME, THE FROG

January, 2003

I was working as Vice President of Operations during the day, only to be treated as a doormat at night. You know when they say that if you throw a frog into a pot of boiling water, it will jump right out, not wanting anything to do with that environment? But if you put the frog in a pot of cold water, put it on the stove and turn on the heat, the frog will adjust and adjust until it is dead. I think the same thing happens with women sometimes; if we went out on a first date and the guy slapped us across the face, chances are we wouldn't go back for seconds. But as it is with abusers, they gradually turn on the heat until one day, you find yourself sitting on the bathroom floor sobbing into your dogs fur, trying to figure out how this could have happened to you.

I was that frog. The heat was now fully turned on and after 14 years, the water was boiling.

Finally, the pain became greater than my fear of being alone. On February 11th, 2003, after receiving absolute evidence about his infidelities, I filed for divorce (I had tried that a couple of years earlier but ended up backing down, incapable of coping with the onslaught from his end). I knew that I was in for one hell of a fight, especially after he threatened to kill me, but I had no choice.

I do not regret the marriage to Mr. X. It taught me so much about life, and about myself. The most important lesson is that I had it right from the beginning. My instincts were talking, no; yelling at me to stay away. I just didn't listen.

# DIVINE DESTINY

Because I thought that the kind of love I was dreaming of couldn't possibly exist, I easily resigned myself to living on a ranch in Montana, surrounded by every 3-legged dog, starving cat, blind horse and geriatric mule looking for a home. I had gone on a couple of cattle drives in Montana and absolutely fell in love with the Big Sky Country!

It took God exactly six days to make my dreams come true. Frank called me on Feb. 17th, asking me to explain a joke that I had sent him for Christmas. Then he asked how I was doing and I told him about the divorce.

"I'm so sorry, Juliette, I didn't see that one coming. Are you ok?" He asked.

"Yes, I am. I'm fine," I lied, sitting on top of the stairs in our Beverly Hills mansion with a 500,000 volt stun baton in my hand, a 375 pound body guard sitting in the living room, waiting for the police to arrive.

"What are you doing on Friday?" Frank asked. I almost dropped the phone. Dead silence. I didn't have a clue what he meant and what I should say.

"The reason I ask, is that I'm invited to Ed Gold's 75th Birthday Party in Palm Springs and I'd like you to go with me. You remember him from the Puck days, don't you?" The only noise was my bodyguard's ass moving a few inches on the leather couch. My mind was racing a buzillion miles a second. *Go to a party? With Frank? Why?! How? As what?*

"Sure, I'd love to." I finally gagged out.

"Terrific! I'll call you in a couple of days and we'll figure out the details. Take care." Click.

Mr. Bodyguard looked up and asked if everything was alright. "I think so," I mumbled, mouth-breathing. I immediately called Micki.

# MICKI

I met Micki in 1990, right after I moved to LA. I responded to an employment ad in the paper and after talking with her on the phone, was told to get into her office right away, she wanted to meet me in person.

I walked into her office on Wilshire Boulevard and was lead to her office which was the size of a small ballroom.

There she was, blonde, gorgeous, her slim and trim body in Chanel while her feet, clad in something fabulous, were resting in the middle of her beautifully polished desk. I was sitting quietly in a comfy chair across from her, while she excitedly talked about investing in an African Gold Mine.

I coughed a few times, but she just waved her heavily bejeweled hand at me, hushing me up.

Finally, she got off the phone. She was about to say something but I beat her to it.

"First of all, that was rather rude. Second, I want in on that deal."

She tilted her head and gave me a powerful, assessing sideways glance. Then something in her eyes lit up and she sat up straight, pulling her sexy legs off her desk.

"You got balls. I like it!" She said, beaming.

"Thanks," I replied, grinning back at her.

Not only did she cut me in on the deal, but we became instant best friends! The deal went sour and died, but our sweet friendship will last a lifetime.

# FIRST DATE

---

"You are not going to believe what just happened!" I yelled into Micki's ear.

"What?" She asked. I told her.

"Do you think this is like a mentor-thing? You know, a "let me lend you a shoulder to lean on because you're a nice person and I want to help?" I asked my friend.

"You're out of your mind!" Micki screamed, like she always does when she gets excited. Then she giggled. "Oh my God, this is great! You've been telling me for years what a great guy this is. I'm so excited!!!"

"When can you come over?" I asked, "I need help picking out clothes."

"I'll be there tomorrow night. This is great. I love this. This is a good thing, Juliette. God is giving you exactly what you asked for!" I hung up the phone, astonished by her declaration, my heart beating just a little faster.

After we chose the right clothes for me to take to Palm Springs, Micki and I sat down with a glass of wine. "What was that dream you had that one time about Frank?" she asked.

"Oh my God, I can't believe you remember that!" I replied.

A couple of years after Frank and I left the Wolfgang Puck Food Company I had this dream. A very vivid dream. It was so real in fact that I ended up writing the whole thing down. The next morning, I read it and thought it was way too cool and profound not to share. I called Frank and left him a voice mail:

"Hi Frank, it's Juliette. I just have to tell you that I had the strangest dream about us last night. No, not that kind of dream! You were living in Boston and called me, saying that I had to come to Boston to work on a project with you. I booked a flight and then saw myself walking up a cobblestone walk way, which lead to your house, which looked sort of like an old fort. After saying hello, you asked me to follow you down into the wine cellar. We sat down, you opened a bottle of wine, pouring it into two glasses and handed me a fork. You said that it was very important to stir this wine with a fork prior to drinking it. Don't ask – I have no idea what that means. Then you handed me a pad of paper and a pen, taking one of each for yourself. You proceeded to tell me that our mission was to come up with a statement explaining what love is. That's all. We worked and worked, wrote and erased, until I excitedly came up with it. I had it! You asked me what it was and here it goes: "Love is the complete and utter acceptance of the person today, with eager anticipation of where growth may take them tomorrow." So there! Thought you should know. Have a great day, bye."

This statement, by the way, was featured on our wedding invitation.

Frank responded a few days later, blown away by the dream and concluding that the statement was in fact a very beautiful description of love.

I drove to Palm Springs that Friday, driving myself bananas wondering what might happen. *This definitely is a mentor thing,* I kept thinking. *I mean, there was never any kind of romantic notion between us. What if it is a romantic thing?! Oh my God, what if he kisses me and there's no chemistry? Oh, and yeah, what if he kisses me and there is??? No, this has to be a friendship / mentor thing. It's got to be. Right?*

Right... When I got to the hotel, Frank was sitting by the pool, a nice bottle of red wine and two glasses in front of him, looking manly and sexy as hell. *Crap. Doesn't look like a mentor-thing.* We talked about the last 3 years, carefully avoiding anything too personal.

We met Ed Gold and his family at Jillian's, a nice restaurant in Palm Springs. I had on tight, yet classy black pants and a gorgeous white sweater. The waiter poured a very nice cabernet, we toasted to Ed, and I was just about to take my first sip when Irvin, one of Ed's sons asked me a question. My hand never got the message and while I looked up, it kept going down – pouring the entire glass right over my white sweater. I knew that dropping the f-bomb from the top of my lungs would not be appropriate, so while everyone was generously ignoring what just happened, I stuffed my white linen napkin into the V-neck of my sweater, looking and feeling like a big fat stupid.

"You look like you could use a cigarette," Frank whispered in my ear. *Ya think?* He didn't wait for a response, got up and pulled my chair back, allowing me and my new best friend dangling from my throat to leave the table. "We'll be right back", he said to the Gold family, who could not have handled the situation in a nicer way.

I concentrated on not hauling ass out the door when I felt Frank's hand grab mine. *Definitely no mentor-thing.* We made it outside and I think I sucked the entire cigarette into my lungs in one, long drag, looking absolutely miserable.

"Don't worry," Frank said trying not to bust a gut, you look fine." I really must have looked miserable and downright pathetic, because Frank continued:

"Juliette, with a face like yours, there's no way people look at anything else." I was sincerely hoping that he wasn't referring to my big nose.

"I'm sorry. This is really embarrassing." I mumbled.

"No it's not – accidents happen. Let's go have a great dinner, shall we?" We walked back to the table, me defiantly glaring at the patrons, silently daring them to stare anywhere but my face!

After a few glasses of wine, all of which landed in the right place, I started to relax and feel better, enjoying the company of the Gold's. By the time we left, I couldn't wait to see them again the next day, at the official party, wearing black.

We drove back in my Jag XJR, listening to "The Prayer" by Celine Dion and Andrea Bocelli, me wondering what would happen next. We didn't even get through the door before Frank threw me against the wall and kissed me like I've never been kissed before. *Holy Mother of God! Who is this man?!* The last coherent thought I remember was: *I'm home.*

The next year was tough. Every month, we spent a weekend together either in LA or in Boston. It always hurt when Frank left on Sunday nights, but one particular time I actually had to pull over because I thought I was having a heart attack. The pain in my heart was excruciating. We had just finished a fantastic dinner at Sushi Roku when I asked him:

"How much are you going to miss me?"

He took me in his arms, looked into my eyes and said "I love you."

The next day, I made an appointment with a hypnotherapist to quit smoking. I couldn't continue to subject the man who loved me to my stinky breath! A few days later I walked out of her office and never had another cigarette.

Little did I know back then how important hypnotism would become in my life.

# BOSTON, HERE WE COME

---

December 12, 2003

It was exactly eleven degrees out and snowing when Magie, my black chow chow and I arrived at Logan International Airport. I'm not sure who was more appalled, he or I. Neither one of us had appropriate attire and were frozen solid by the time we got into Frank's car. I made a mental note to go shopping immediately.

Since Frank lived in a penthouse condo in Chestnut Hills that didn't allow dogs, I had rented a carriage house not too far away. Frank might as well have sold the condo right then and there because he never went back to his "hooch" again...

First thing the next morning, I took Magie out for a walk. Frozen half to death I soon saw a little trail of blood in his paw-prints. We turned around immediately and before I went to buy gloves, hats, scarves, electric socks and ugly boots for myself, I ran to Petco and bought little red leather booties for Magie. His little feet had never been exposed to anything but meticulously manicured Beverly Hills lawns.

Frank came home that night and almost snorted himself out the door.

"What is that?!" He asked, pointing at Magie's red booted feet.

"That, my friend, is protective gear from this frozen hell ground you call home!" I explained.

No matter how hard Frank tried to persuade me that Magie was "just" a dog and would get used to frozen rocks and ice, I kept those booties on him for the rest of the winter.

It was a particularly cold morning and I, who'd been fighting a cold for weeks, did not want to get out of bed.

"Honey, would you mind taking Magie out for a quick walk before you go to work?" I asked, sweetly.

"Sure, no problem", and off they went.

I was snug and cozy and warm when Frank stuck his head into the bedroom.

"Uh, JouJou, you might want to get up and take care of Magie. He got skunked."

"He got what?" I asked, drowsy from sleep.

"Skunked. On his head. I'm sorry but I have to run." Kiss kiss and bye bye.

I got up and found my baby downstairs. I didn't know what "skunked" meant and was leaning in for a hug when I almost puked on his already wet head.

Urgh and yuck and double yuck. Are you kidding me? Off to Petco we went, this time together, with all the windows and the roof open, in the middle of a blizzard. I told them to please do whatever it took to get the stench off of him. Then I drove home and burned my clothes.

# HI NAHANT

March 2004

Frank took me out to the Top of the Hub for dinner and I realized, for the first time, that Boston was surrounded by water. Everywhere I looked, there was water.

"Frank, since my lease at the carriage house is up soon, let's look for a place with a water view".

"I don't know if we can find something we like that's affordable, honey – but let's see what's out there anyway."

I called Coldwell Banker's and asked for the best realtor in the North Shore, and the South Shore. A couple of hours later, I was on the phone with Eleanor. She showed me fifteen properties in the North Shore, all of which had water views. I liked five of them and showed them to Frank.

"Call Eleanor and tell her that if she can find a place with the layout of this property, the commute from that property, the privacy of the other one and the square footage of that one, to give us a call." *Great*, I thought, *we'll never hear from her again.*

Two days later she called and said that she remembered a house that had everything we were looking for. It had been for sale in 2002 but financing fell through at the last moment. They were putting it back on the market tomorrow.

"Eleanor, I will meet you there in 45 minutes" I yelled, flying out the door.

The minute I was on the causeway to Nahant I knew that this was a magical place. Then I walked into the house and totally lost it.

"This is incredible! I mean, absolutely amazing!" I exclaimed, red faced, jumping up and down beyond thrilled. Since the owners were home, Eleanor advised me to keep my excitement down a bit. I failed miserably.

"Judy, this is Juliette. Is Frank there?" I asked Frank's assistant.

"Yes he is but he is in a meeting."

"This is an emergency. You have to pull him out."

"Ok, just a minute."

"Juliette, are you ok?" Frank asked, worried. I had never pulled him out of a meeting before.

"Yes, I am. I am doing great. Hey, do you want to see the house before you buy it?" I asked.

"Um yes, I'd like to, very much actually," Frank said, a bit confused.

"Ok then. Honey, you have to cancel whatever meeting you're in and get in your car and come to Nahant. Right now. They are putting the house back on the market tomorrow and you have to see it now!"

"Give me the address, I'm on my way." My man of action!

I was impatiently waiting for Frank's arrival. As soon as he stepped out of the car, I excitedly grabbed his hand and began showing him around.

"Frank, LOOK! This is absolutely incredible, isn't it? I mean, look at this view. And, it's fenced in and totally private. And it's only 25 minutes from Boston. It's exactly what we wanted! And by the way, say hi to the Parisi's, the owners."

After politely saying hi to Joe and Barbara, Frank pulled me aside and asked me, also very politely, to keep my excitement down a bit. It didn't work coming from him, either…

We thanked the Parisi's and left, Frank behind Eleanor, me behind Frank. I called him immediately.

"Frank, this house is perfect, isn't it? I mean, it has every single thing we wanted, and then some. We can't wait until tomorrow and end up in a bidding war. We have to jump on this now!"

"Ok ok, you're right" Frank admitted, honking and flashing his lights, motioning for Eleanor to pull over. We wrote a low ball offer sitting at Tides, the local Nahant restaurant, and prepared for a price battle. At this point, I felt truly sorry that my excitement was so over the top, especially after Frank and Eleanor pointed out again that turning into a drooling, out of control excited homebuyer in front of the current owners was not the most financially beneficial thing to do.

At 8:35 am the next morning, we got a call from Eleanor.

"You got it. They took your offer. I can't believe it!" She was beside herself. So were we.

"Are you serious? Really? I thought this was going to turn into such a big ordeal due to my idiotic behavior," I said.

"No, on the contrary. They absolutely loved your excitement and your enthusiasm. They love their home very much and want it to go to someone who will truly cherish and appreciate it". Who says you have to play the game?! We moved in April and have loved every single minute living in our magical home.

It was an unusually hot May and Frank looked like a sweaty grunt digging up old roots in the yard. He came in to get an ice cold beer and mumbled something about "stinking heat" and "Vietnam". A few minutes later, the phone rang and it was Doug Hilts, Frank's point man from Vietnam. We immediately scheduled a joyful, yet emotional get-together during which Doug told Frank about the yearly Delta Co, 2/8 1st Cav reunions. Frank respectfully declined, not wanting to wallow in the past. I wasn't having any of that.

"You may not want to go, but I'm going." I said, crawling into bed that night.

"And where is it that you want to go?" he asked, opening his arms.

"To the Vietnam Reunion! If you think that I am passing up on the opportunity to learn more about such an important part of your life, you're out of your head."

Knowing that I was not kidding, Frank said, smiling "ok, I guess we're going. I love you.

# I'M A HYPNOTIST!

After a few weeks of living in our new home, I had a dream.

"Frank?"

"Yes?"

"I had the strangest dream.  I dreamt that I was a hypnotherapist."

"Huh?"

"A hypnotherapist.  You know, somebody who hypnotizes people."

"You know what?  I think that that's a terrific idea.  Do it." Frank said enthusiastically.

"Are you serious?  But, I'm a business woman."

"Juliette, people tell you everything. I've never met anyone who can get people, even complete strangers, to open up the way you get them to do. This will give you the tools to not just listen to them, but to actually help them."

"Hm." I replied, "maybe."

The more I thought about it, the more it started to make sense. I do love people and I do love listening to their stories, problems and worries.

Not one to wait, I called the hypnotherapist who helped me quit smoking in LA and got the information I needed to get going. By October, I was a certified hypnotherapist and opened my business, Center Of Thought. Hypnotism rocked and shook my world. The more dramatic the results, the more I wanted to learn. I went to every National Guild of Hypnotist's convention and took every class I could get my hands on. I got certified in complementary medical hypnotism, and a year later in clinical hypnotism. In 2011, I got a certification in neurolinguistic programming and will go for my masters in 2012. Little did I know what a role all this would play in the crisis to come.

Life with Frank was amazing. My entire life I had hoped and prayed for a love like this, and now it was mine. We never fought, never had an argument and were never disrespectful towards one another. Not to this day. Early on we decided to put our relationship first. Not him, not me. If one person wins, the other loses, and so does the relationship. So we put our egos, our need to be right, to bed from the very beginning and it has worked out beautifully.

After a draining four and a half year divorce, I was finally free to marry the love of my life.

# A PURPLE EGG BEFORE THE WEDDING

Saturday, July 7th, 2007

Leave it to me to blow just about every tendon and ligament in my left ankle one week before my wedding! As they say: be careful what you wish for. It's not that I wished to blow the ankle, but Frank and I fantasized about a cozy little wedding on the beach, me barefoot wearing a simple white dress. The barefoot part was definitely happening.

My sister Rita, Frank's sister Joanna and her daughter Gina, along with our neighbors and very good friends Roz and Comare were at the house, helping me put together the center pieces for the wedding tables. I was carrying the left over candles back into the house when the screen door slammed shut, trapping the sole of my sandal. I had a choice to either fall forward onto my face (not a good idea) or to twist sideways and land on my side (much better idea). I was laying there gulping down every bad word I could think of when Roz came in and sat down next to me.

"Are you ok"?

"No. Not ok. Not ok at all. OUCH!"

Within the next few moments all the girls were around me, none of them too surprised. I had blown the very same ankle about a year prior, slipping on some lamb juice that dripped off my plate. Back then, Frank told me to walk it off, since that was what you did as an athlete or a soldier… It didn't work back then and I was not about to try it now. I watched as a gigantic purple egg started to form on the outside of the ankle, matching the big scab on my knee, where a week ago I managed to trip and fall over a pebble walking Magie.

Frank came downstairs to find out what the commotion was all about. He saw me laying there, looking rather pathetic, and smiled!

"I had a feeling something like this would happen. Actually, it was just a matter of time".

"You did? It was? What do you mean?" I asked, stifling a sob.

Kneeling by my side, eyes full of twinkles and adoring amusement, he said: "Honey, you're not exactly Miss Graceful. Let me help you up." He carried me outside onto a chair, my foot landing smack dab in the center of the table. A few minutes later Andy, Roz' husband, came over. He took a look at the foot and decided that I should stick it into a tub of ocean water. No problem since the ocean is right in front of our house. Before I could voice my concerns, Andy grabbed a bucket and walked down our ramp to the ocean, scooping up a few gallons. I was trying to be very brave, sitting there with my foot submerged in salt water and seaweed. Once in a while, somebody would grab my foot, look at the ever growing egg, and stick it back in the bucket. About three hours went by and it did not get better, and I was sick and tired of being brave.

"Frank, we have to go to the emergency room."

"You think so?" He replied.

"I do. I think so very much."

We said goodbye to our friends and headed to Brigham and Women's in Boston. I held my leg up in the air because it hurt to put it down. I was in pain and Frank stepped on the gas, to be pulled over immediately by a cop. I think the cop was finishing a box of donuts because it took him forever to get out of the car! Frank tried to get out once to get his attention, but got yelled at to get back inside the car. So we waited. Finally, the cop came over and before he opened his mouth, I screamed: "Look! Please, look at my leg. I think I broke my ankle and need to get to the emergency room." The cop not only backed off, but stopped traffic to let us back on the road, mumbling something about us driving carefully.

The doctor looked at the X-rays and gave me a pill. "No walking for two weeks, then take it easy for another four, ok?"

"No. Not ok. We're getting married next Saturday." He was about to put a really ugly cast on my foot when Frank said: "Seriously, Doc, you expect her to wear that thing with a wedding gown?" By the time we left, my foot was featuring a beautiful white air cast. But this was nothing compared to what loomed ahead.

# SAVED BY THE MOB

---

A Beach Wedding

The part about our wedding being on the beach should not have been a problem since we pretty much live on the beach. We had just sent out the "Save the Date" card, which featured a picture of a beautiful beach with little footprints in the sand. Just when we thought that all was set and done, I received a call from town hall giving us all kinds of new and unexpected conditions: No parking on the beach. No glassware on the beach. No music past 9:00 pm and no bright lights. *Crap – how can we have a wedding like that?!* I was beyond upset and called Comare: "You are NOT going to believe this!" I yelled, telling her the whole story, seeing our wedding turn into one big, fat disaster.

"Give me five minutes, Julio," click.

About a minute later, she called back: "I called Barbara and you're having your wedding at the Angiulo Estate." She said matter of factly.

"We are? How? Why? Why would she do that for us?" I was stunned.

"Because she likes you and because she lives for a good party," was the simple reply. It goes without saying that Barbara is also a terrific lady who's always ready to lend a helping hand.

I immediately called Frank: "Honey, we're having a Mob wedding!"

"Come again?"

I told him what happened and he found the change of venue just terrific.

Barbara Angiulo was Jerry Angiulo's wife. Jerry used to be the "Godfather" here in New England, in charge of the Italian Mob. He was still doing time at that point and Barbara was free to rule the roost. Two weeks after our wedding, Jerry was released from prison. Had that happened prior to our wedding, we would have been back at the beach eating off paper plates and slurping bubbly from plastic cups, in the dark with no music.

THE HAPPIEST PEOPLE DON'T NECESSARILY HAVE THE BEST OF EVERYTHING; THEY JUST MAKE THE MOST OF EVERYTHING THAT COMES THEIR WAY. HAPPINESS LIES FOR THOSE WHO CRY, THOSE WHO HURT, THOSE WHO HAVE SEARCHED, AND THOSE WHO HAVE TRIED. FOR ONLY THEY CAN APPRECIATE THE IMPORTANCE OF PEOPLE WHO HAVE TOUCHED THEIR LIVES.

**Author Unknown**

# PRE-WEDDING LAUGHS

Friday, July 13th, 2007

I was deliriously happy. My foot was wrapped in an ice cold, egg white soaked cabbage leaf and stuck in a towel. That is not why I was so happy, though. I was surrounded by my entire family who all flew in from Switzerland. Bernie, my oldest sister, arrived a couple of days early with her very handsome boys Manuel and Silvio. My mom and dad arrived the day before and along with them came a litany of good old Swiss remedies. They immediately got busy with my foot. Rita, the middle sister, along with her husband Jurgen and their also very good looking boys Samuel and Michaja, had already been here for a week.

Rita is a very interesting woman. She devoted her life to Christ in her early teens and has become a dedicated missionary. At some point she spent seven years in England, assisting in the translation of the bible into the Mongolian language. After this accomplishment, she and Jurgen, along with their two little boys, ventured out to Mongolia and worked there as missionaries for thirteen years. When they got to the capitol, Ulaanbaatar, there was not a single church. When they left, there were around 150! One day, I called her from Beverly Hills. They were renting a tiny apartment and the heat had gone out yet again. The entire family was sitting in bed, wearing every piece of clothing they had including gloves and hats, covered with every blanket they could find. I think it was about thirty degrees below zero. Rita lives an extremely frugal life, extremely conscientious of every penny she spends.

Little by little my best friends arrived. Making an entrance and walking into our home like she owned the place was Micki. While Micki is in her element sitting at the Ritz, sipping Veuve Clicquot, nibbling on caviar while making a killer deal on the phone, she is also a devoted Christian. She takes no prisoners when it comes to business, but will absolutely give you the shirt off her back if you need it. In 2009, her son Anthony dove into the ocean in Miami and broke his neck. Since admitting him to Project Walk in California, Micki has spent every possible minute building her foundation "Walking with Anthony" to help paralyzed people pay for rehab. She personally has spent hundreds of thousands of dollars helping patients. Her faith is unshakable and she's one hell of a woman!

Then my buddy Moira arrived, the brilliant yet goofy friend we all need. We met working at Nestle in 1993. Moira has a heart of gold and has always been there for me. No matter how big or trivial my problems were, I could always count on my American big sister to put a positive spin on them. Moira and I spent hours reciting the Jerky Boys, laughing ourselves sick, while annoying the hell out of everyone around us. Frank happened to be in the car with the two of us one time when we had a fit of Jerky-mania. After about an hour or so, instead of flinging himself out of the driving car, he ended up joining the insanity. Nobody ever has been able to do that! Of all my friends, Moira is probably the most protective of me and I like it.

And finally, my "girlfriend" Doug arrived. Doug is not gay, not gay at all, but he was always by my side through thick and thin, ever since we worked at Hornblower Yachts in San Francisco back in 1988. He's been listening to me bitch and moan and complain for years, just like a good girlfriend does!

In the afternoon, we went over to the Angiulo Estate to go over the ceremony. My bridesmaids (mom, Bernie, Rita, Joanna, Micki and Moira) were finally "yelled" into the right spot. It was so windy we couldn't hear ourselves think, never mind communicate with each other! Frank and I were worried about the next day and what would happen if this wind didn't subside. He was just asking our sound guy to bring a few extra speakers, when out of nowhere Micki grabbed my arm and said: "Which one is your missionary sister?" I pointed to Rita and followed a determined Micki over there.

"Rita?" Micki asked as she grabbed Rita's hands. Now picture this. Micki in a magnificent designer outfit and killer heels, adorned with about a half a million dollars worth of jewelry. She is as confident and self assured as no human being has a right to be. Rita, on the other hand, is rather shy and somewhat demure, trying her best never to be the center of attention.

"Uh, yes?" Rita cautiously replied, looking mildly shocked and very surprised as her hands were lifted high into the air by Micki's.

"Hey, I'm Micki."

"Lord!" Micki screamed over the wind. "We are gathered here today in preparation for Juliette and Frank's wedding tomorrow. Now, we are NOT going to have this wind tomorrow. You said that if two people gather in the name of your son Jesus, their prayer will be answered. So we are asking, Lord! No wind tomorrow. This we ask and pray for in the name of Jesus Christ, your son, Amen!" Micki dropped Rita's hands, turned on her 4" heels and asked me where the champagne was. I will never, ever forget the look on Rita's face, gaping after Micki's departing, swaying little butt, then at her hands which were still floating in the air.

The laughter continued during dinner at the Revere UNO, where we were joined by more friends and family. Bernie, whom I love with every fiber of my being, looks as much as my sister as a mouse looks like a moose. She's a tiny blonde with blue eyes. I'm a giraffe and dark. Bernie is probably the most positive, warm hearted and spontaneous person I know. She has been supportive no matter how many times we've changed course. Every time I need absolute enthusiasm for anything I do, she's the one I call. Bernie is also rather, shall I say, innocent to social etiquette? So there we were, enjoying dinner. Seated next to Bernie was one of Frank's all time best friends, Ed Gold. To describe Ed is like trying to describe sunlight. He used to be a lawyer, then a judge in New York City. 78 years old and he looks like Tarzan. He has more charm than Cary Grant, Rock Hudson, Sean Connery and Frank Sinatra combined! Ed is one of the most distinguished, polished gentlemen I've ever met. To know Ed is to love Ed.

"Bernie, you have to try this breadstick" I said, sitting across the table from her. "Ed, would you mind passing her one?"

Ed carefully grabbed a breadstick with his napkin and handed it to Bernie. I was about to take a bite of my salad when I watched in absolute horror, how Bernie slid her chair back and leaned way down to take a huge bite right off the breadstick. She scooted her chair back in and gleefully declared "yummy"! Frank and I looked at Ed, who was staring at the half bitten off piece of bread in his hand. I could see every synapse in Ed's brain firing; he must have gone over ten different scenarios as to how to best handle this situation. I'm sure one option was to throw the stick into Bernie's bread plate with a quiet YUCK on his lips. Instead, he took a huge bite off the other end and, leaning towards Bernie, crooned: "Yummy is right!" Bernie proudly smiled until she looked up at Frank and me. "What?!" she asked. If Frank hadn't been CEO of UNO, I'm pretty sure we'd have been thrown out that night.

The importance of these friends becomes so very clear in what was to come.

# A WEDDING DREAM COMES TRUE

Saturday, July 14th, 2007

The wedding was spectacular! The temperature was in the mid seventies and behold, there was absolutely no wind! Our wedding guests were seated behind the pool, the ceremony was taking place in front of the pool, which was in front of the ocean. Frank, his son Will and my dad were standing to the right, downtown Boston gleaming in the background. Magie was snoring lazily at Will's feet.

Mom made her entrance and lined up on the left, followed by Bernie, Rita, Joanna, Micki and Moira. The song "Love to be Loved by You" by Mark Terenzi was gently playing in the background.

It was the happiest day of my life and the joy in my heart countered the pain in my foot. Still, I was leaning pretty heavily on my dad as we were walking "down the aisle".

The happiest day of my life!

From left to right: Moira, Bernie, Mom, Me, Rita, Joanna and Micki

Frank's and my eyes met and the sparks that flew between us could be seen around the world, I'm sure! It was a beautiful, short ceremony held by our reverend Larry Titus. When it was time for our vows, Frank looked at me with so much love in his eyes and said the following words:

"This is what we will do: Love the earth, the sun and the animals. Love each other, our families and friends. We will stand up for those that are challenged, stand against tyrants, the self-absorbed and those that are consumed by materialism. We will have patience for all those who care and know commitment, accept God and most importantly, have patience with each other; and our life will be a great poem."

I had something prepared myself but couldn't get a word out. My beaming smile, drowned by a stream of tears, spoke for itself. Then, we played "The Prayer" by Celine Dion and Josh Groban for all to enjoy.

When Larry pronounced us husband and wife, I threw myself into Frank's arms for a not-so-wifely-kiss, and then leaned down to pet Magie who'd woken up and loudly declared: "Magie, we're Italian!" The festivities were underway and almost a year of absolute bliss followed. And then it started.

# FRANK TURNS YELLOW

Thursday, June 12th, 2008

"Honey, you look yellow," I said, staring at Frank who was reading yet another ever-so-fascinating book like "Salt," "Cod," or "Goat Song."

"Huh?"

"Frank, seriously, you're yellow. Your skin, your eyeballs – they're yellow." He glanced up trying to figure out if I was serious.

"You sure?"

"YES! Go look in the mirror." He got up and padded from our bed into the bathroom. I heard him grunt something and before I knew it, he was back in bed, his nose buried in his book, mumbling something about making an appointment with Dr. Abramson in the morning. Soon after, we fell asleep wrapped in each other's arms. I was going back and forth between wondering why my husband was yellow, and how much fun we would have in Nantucket, celebrating our first wedding anniversary on July 14th.

Friday, June 13th, 2008

"How did it go? What did he say?" I asked Frank, handing him a Belvedere Martini, extra dry with three olives, sticking my nose up to his lips to get my "honey I'm home kiss." Dr. Abramson, as always, had made himself available that very same day.

"You were right, I'm jaundiced. Not sure yet what's causing it, but Dr. Abramson said that it's most likely a gallbladder stone that's lodged in the gallbladder duct, causing the bile to back up and excrete out into the blood stream. He did all kinds of blood work. I'm scheduled for an Ultrasound on June 16th to see if I have stones."

"I wonder if that has anything to do with that weird stomach flu you've been having," I said. Since the beginning of May, Frank experienced stomach flu like symptoms, plus his stool was dark, oily, stinky and floating. There were times I was amazed that my nose didn't fall off in self defense.

"Maybe. Probably. That makes sense," he agreed. "That's why I felt so shitty in Italy." Frank, his COO Roger Zingle and Executive Chef Chris Gatto, were invited to visit Casa Della Buitoni the beginning of June, and he was so looking forward to enjoying the great food over there. Instead, he felt bloated, crampy, weak and miserable the whole time. Whenever he called and mentioned those symptoms, I felt like telling him to take an Advil, grab a box of chocolates and jump into a warm bath with a fashion magazine...

## Monday, June 16th, 2008

The ultrasound didn't show any stone accumulation in the gallbladder, but we were still pretty sure that one of them was stuck in the duct. Dr. Abramson arranged for Frank to get an MRCP at Newton Wellesley Hospital. MRCP stands for Magnetic Resonance Cholangiopancreatography, in medical imaging, a technique to visualize the biliary tract and pancreatic ducts. I was not at all worried. My grandfather had a kidney stone once and it was no big deal. A stone is a stone, right? I remember joking about making a piece of jewelry out of the stone, depending on the clarity and quality of it.

## Wednesday, June 18th, 2008

The MRCP didn't show any stones either. Next step: an ERCP: Endoscopic Retrograde Cholangiopancreatography, a technique that combines the use of endoscopy and fluoroscopy to diagnose and treat certain problems of the biliary or pancreatic ductal systems. Through the endoscope, the physician can see the inside of the stomach and duodenum, and inject dyes into the ducts in the biliary tree and pancreas to they can be seen on x-rays.

# NO SMOKING GUN

Wednesday, June 25th, 2008

Because it is obvious that we are totally and insanely in love with each other, the head nurse at Newton Wellesley came to get me immediately after the ERCP, allowing me to be by Frank's bedside when he woke up in the recovery room. I was stroking his beautiful salt and pepper hair and every few minutes, he woke up and said "ok, I'm ready, let's go." Then he'd fall right back to sleep. At some point, the doctor showed up and asked me to follow him into a conference room. That was the first time I felt a flutter of fear. He started to draw a picture of the liver, gallbladder, the stomach and the pancreas, and told me that they did not find the "smoking gun," the stone. His guess was that Frank might have Pancreatitis, some form of infection of the pancreas. That could easily be dealt with by taking antibiotics and/or some surgical removal of the affected area of the pancreas. But what needed to be done first, through another ERCP, was to put a stent into Frank's common bile duct to prevent the bile from backing up any further. *Ok, we can deal with that*, I thought. I went back to Frank's bedside and watched my love wake up.

The second time I started to feel uncomfortable was when all the nurses came to say good bye to us. They looked into my eyes in a way that spoke volumes, saying: "good luck to you." It was not the typical "hey, nice to meet you and good luck." It was a very serious, meaningful "Good Luck to You" and I knew that they knew that something might be very wrong. What, I had no idea.

A couple of hours later, we were sitting in a restaurant called D'Parma in Winthrop, having lunch. Frank and I were still not too worried, because you see, Frank's a total stud and healthy as a horse. I mean, here's a man, 6'2", 200 lbs of solid muscle, who eats healthy (or so we thought back then) and works out every day. Whatever this was, we'd deal with it quickly and effectively.

# MORE TESTS AND A CARING DOCTOR

Monday, June 30th, 2008

We're back at Newton Wellesley for yet another ERCP, a stent placement and a needle biopsy of the pancreas. We were both hoping that this would be the last time we'd see the inside of a hospital for a while. Enough already. So we put on our happy faces and courageously did what had to be done.

I had a physical with my primary care physician, Dr. Maury McGough, a few days earlier. She is one of those fabulous doctors who actually sits down and talks to you and listens to what you have to say. I told her what was going on with Frank, and she said: "Juliette, I would really like for you to get a second opinion. The best guy is Dr. David Rattner at Mass General, he is the Chief of the Division of General and Gastrointestinal Surgery and this is who I would go to. Let me contact him and get you an appointment for Frank, ok?" Like I said – she's amazing.

The next few days were pretty uneventful. I was a little worried about the pancreatitis thing and how we could schedule that surgery, if needed, around our anniversary in Nantucket. The big decision of the day was whether we'd stay in a cute, romantic little B&B, or the White Elephant.

# YEAH!  ONLY A-TYPICAL CELLS!

---

Wednesday, July 2nd, 2008

Frank came home early and we enjoyed one of my fabulous dinners – I think it was Osso Bucco with creamed spinach and Kamut pasta.  I love to cook and Frank is the best person in the world to cook for.  He loves everything I dish out and then asks for seconds and thirds.  We had just finished our dinner when the call came from Newton Wellesley.

"We have great news.  You have nothing to worry about.  The biopsy revealed only a-typical cells so nothing else needs to be done at this point!"

Yippee!!!  We opened a bottle of Silver Oak Cabernet, my favorite, and went for a long walk around our beloved island, Nahant.  We held hands and celebrated life.  We were clear and free and all was just the way it should be. We went home and made love, two hearts beating to the sound of relief.

# YOU HAVE PANCREATIC CANCER

Thursday, July 3rd, 2008

Dr. McGough arranged for us to see Dr. Rattner today. Even though we knew that Frank was okay, we didn't want to cancel because Dr. McGough went out of her way to get us that appointment.

I have this "thing" when I meet doctors for the first time. I always try to look my best because I want them to take me seriously. So I prepared for this appointment by throwing on Gucci, Chanel and Prada. I was ready to be taken seriously. We entered the Wang Building and headed to the 4th floor, Suite 460. After checking in, Frank was handed a pile of paperwork to fill out while I was looking around the room. The first thing I saw was a big sign on the wall:

## DIVISION OF GENERAL AND
## GASTROINTESTINAL SURGERY

MASSACHUSETTS GENERAL HOSPITAL      MASSACHUSETTS GENERAL HOSPITAL
DIGESTIVE HEALTHCARE      CENTER  CANCER CENTER

COLORECTAL SURGERY PROGRAM
ENDOCRINE SURGERY PROGRAM
GASTROESOPHAGEAL SURGERY PROGRAM
LIVER SURGERY PROGRAM
PANCREAS / BILIARY SURGERY PROGRAM

The only word I saw was Cancer.  I looked around, noticing all kinds of people in the waiting area and thought, *oh my God, some of these people must have cancer.* Then I turned to help Frank with the paperwork.

The first cold fist of fear closed around my heart when I saw the following sentence on one of the forms:  *"Is there anything specific you wish to talk to your oncologist about today?"*  ONCOLOGIST.  Why were we seeing an oncologist?!  What was THAT word doing on Frank's intake form?

"Frank, why are we seeing an oncologist?" I asked with a shaky voice.

"That's probably standard wording for these forms, honey.  We are not seeing an oncologist, but we're in the same division of the hospital that takes care of cancer patients, don't worry."  But I did.

Frank dropped the papers off at the front desk, and a few short minutes later, we were asked to come meet Dr. Rattner.  Beside Dr. Rattner was an obviously pregnant, young and beautiful woman in a lab coat; I assumed she was an Intern or something like that.  He introduced her as Dr. Cristina Ferrone.  *Wow, she's a doctor,* I thought.  We went over Frank's medical history which they had already accessed in their computer system, which is linked to Newton Wellesley's. I ended the recap by beamingly stating "the good news is that Frank has no problems anymore. We got a call from Newton Wellesley last night and all it was and is are a-typical cells!"

Cristina looked at us and dropped the nuclear bomb.

"I'm 99% sure that we're dealing with Pancreatic Cancer here." She stated, calmly.

Oncologist. Cancer. Frank? The next few moments are a blur, but I do remember Frank giving me one of those amazing looks that says: *it's ok baby, we can handle it.* I dumbfoundedly stared at both doctors when Frank said: "so what's the plan?"

"Dr. Ferrone is one of the best gastrointestinal surgeons in this country, and she specializes in Pancreatic Cancer," Dr. Rattner declared.

*Her?* I thought? *No way, we want the best.*

"Dr. Rattner, since Dr. Maury McGough arranged for us to meet with you, I would like you to be my surgeon," Frank said.

"Well, my back can't handle these long surgeries any more, but I can assure you that Dr. Ferrone is a highly respected, well known surgeon and you will be in the best of hands with her," he replied.

*Just how long of a surgery was he talking about,* I wondered.

As I turned to look at the young, beautiful Dr. Ferrone, I could see in her eyes that this was not the first time she was subjected to being questioned as a surgeon. It's almost as if she expected it – but there was no resentment or irritation in her eyes. All I saw was absolute confidence.

"I want to run my own tests, with my own team," Dr. Ferrone said. "Once we confirm that it is Pancreatic Cancer, we will decide on how to proceed and whether Frank qualifies for the Whipple."

*The Whipple? That sounded like a luscious ice cream sundae, how bad could a Whipple be?*

Staring at her huge pregnant belly, I blurted out: "At least we know you won't be drunk or hung-over during the surgery."

Frank gave me the most incredulous look, and then we all started laughing; I think Dr. Ferrone would have doubled over had her belly not been in the way. As it turns out, the Whipple is one of the most complicated surgeries. They literally remodel your insides. They remove the head of the pancreas and all the shared blood supplies and blood structures to other organs. In addition, they remove a piece of the stomach, the bile duct, a piece of the small bowel as well as the gallbladder. After that, everything has to be reconnected again; including the small bowel to the pancreas, the bile duct and the stomach.

On our way home, Frank made me promise not to tell anyone, except for immediate family and very, very close friends, after having sworn them to secrecy. Both of our heads were spinning, my stomach hurt, and for once I had no idea what to say or do.

## "THE SUN ALWAYS SHINES. SOME DAYS, YOU JUST CAN'T SEE IT"

### Author Unknown

Wednesday, July 9th, 2008

We cancelled Nantucket and instead headed West on Route 16 to Mass General first thing in the morning for yet another ERCP and an EUS (Endoscopic Ultrasound), this time with Dr. Ferrone's team. We got the call that night confirming Pancreatic Cancer. We were also told that there were two spots on Frank's liver that had to be biopsied. Frank, as always, took me in his arms and told me that everything would be ok.

"People survive cancer all the time sweetie, and I'm going to be one of them."

I cried and prayed my guts out that night.

In the middle of the night, I woke up and not wanting to wake up my love, I grabbed Moose, our ragdoll cat, who'd been peacefully sleeping at my feet. Moose is a gift from God. Really. I am going to tell you the whole story and then I dare you to disagree with me.

# MOOSE

First week in January 08, Bernie and her boyfriend once again broke up. This time he moved out and she was very upset and sad. I suggested that she get a kitten, something to come home to; something she could snuggle with. To my utter amazement, I received an email from her a couple of days later, with pictures of her Maine Coon kitten attached. *Oh my God what a cutie. Want!*

I've always loved cats, but my ex husband made it very clear that I could either have a goldfish or a chow chow. Since goldfish make terrible cuddlers, I opted for the chow chow. I called the AKC and found the perfect breeders, Bob and Love Banghart. They told me that a bitch was about to have a litter and to bring a worn T-Shirt. That's right – they let their dogs pick the people, not the other way around. When a puppy picks the t-shirt he likes best, the owner of that t-shirt gets that particular puppy. The cutest black male picked me and our bond was astounding from the beginning. I adored that dog. Magie Noir, which means black magic in French and is pronounced "Mawshee Newa" and I were inseparable. He was also

81

my sole source of love and affection for many years. While my Ex abhorred my touch, Magie lived for it. I often prayed to God to please, when the time came, to take him home quickly and painlessly. The mere thought of having to hold him while they put him down destroyed me.

As Magie got older, friends suggested that I get another puppy. While Frank thought it a good idea, I couldn't bring myself to bring another dog into the house. I was Magie's and Magie's alone. That is, until Bernie's kitten popped up on my screen. *What about a kitten*, I thought? *A kitten would be perfect company for my aging boy.*

I went online and called every Maine Coon cat breeder in New England. None were home. I continued looking at various breeds and the only other one that caught my breath was the ragdoll. What an amazingly beautiful cat!

"Honey, I almost bought us a cat today" I exclaimed happily after Frank kissed my nose hello.

"Oh yeah? Don't you think that's something we should talk about?" He inquired.

"Ok. Let's talk about it. What do you think?"

"Great idea." He said, grinning at me.

"Well. Am I glad we talked about it!" I answered, beaming.

That night, Frank and I woke up at about 3 am. "Let's talk about a name" I said, looking forward to a fun discussion.

"Moose," came the instant reply.

"What? Moose? Why?" I wanted to know.

"Well, I always liked the name Max. And if we ever get another dog and call him Max, and we have a cat named Moose, we'll have a "MaxiMoose", as in the old Roman gladiator!" This was hysterically funny at 3 a.m. and I went with it, making a mental note to rent Gladiator again.

The next day, instead of stopping by Whole Foods for a quick lunch after our work out, Frank decided to check out a deli he heard much about. He wanted to get some food to go but at the last minute changed his mind and we sat down at a little table at Periwinkles' in Swampscott. On the table next to us was a newspaper, opened at the classified section. I grabbed it and the first thing I saw were the Pet ads. There must have been over 50 puppies for sale, and then, at the bottom, was a lonely ad:

"Ragdoll kitten. Male. Beautiful blue eyes."

"Frank check this out. Let's call them." We did. I explained to the lady that we were considering either a Ragdoll or a Maine Coon, and she burst out laughing.

"Those are two very different animals, Juliette. The coon will take your house apart, shred your curtains and furniture, and demand tons of activities. *Note to self: call Bernie and tell her to hide her furniture.* The ragdoll, also known as the gentle giant, hardly moves. They are completely defenseless, not knowing how to use their teeth or claws. They are the sweetest, most laid back and affectionate cats there are."

My heart skipped a beat as this sounded too good to be true. I wanted a laid back, affectionate gentle giant. Sometimes the stars align. I would need this cat in the days to come.

"Can we come look at him, please" I begged.

"Of course, come on down".

Two hours later we were heading South on I 93 towards Randolph. The minute I saw the kitten, my heart melted, my arms opened, and tears formed in my eyes as I held the soft little fur ball to my chest. Frank, on the other hand, started asking all the right questions about their disposition, food, requirements, proneness to illness, etc. The lady and her husband patiently answered all the questions, all the while knowing that I was a goner. In my arms was a wet nose, four soft legs and a fluffy tail. He was mine!

"Have you thought of a name?" she asked me, turning away from Frank.

"Uhu, yes, actually we have." I replied. She stared at me, waiting.

"Moose. His name is Moose." I said, sheepishly.

She blinked. "Really?"

"Yup. Moose." Frank confirmed.

"That's weird," she answered, looking at her husband. "If we would have kept him, we would have called him Moose, too. You see, his father's name is Max, and we thought it would be kind of funny to have a MaxiMoose."

You could have heard a pin drop. Frank and I looked at each other, me catching my breath, him reaching for the check book. This had to be Divine Intervention! We never explained our reason for wanting to call him Moose, we didn't think they'd believe us. *God, message received. Loud and clear!*

I went to get him a couple of days later, after spending an enormous amount of money at Pet Express to make sure little Moose had all he could ever need and want. I remember singing to him the entire way home, belting out "There's a Time For Us" by Il Divo.

Two weeks later, Magie passed away in his sleep. Frank and I were in St. Patrick's Cathedral, his favorite church in New York, when I got the call from Mary, our "babysitter".

"Juliette, it's Mary. I don't think Magie is breathing." She said, barely breathing herself.

"What do you mean, Mary? Where is he?" I asked, somewhat panicky.

"He is laying on the kitchen floor, he looks like he's sleeping, but he's not breathing." Poor Mary was beside herself.

"It's ok, Mary. Just hang tight. I'll call you right back." I called Comare and asked her to go over to the house. She called back a few minutes later.

"Juliette, he's gone. I'm so sorry." I couldn't believe it. I called Joe and Barbara Parisi, our dear friends whom we bought our house from. Joe owns the Marblehead Animal Hospital and has been Magie's vet for years.

"Joe, I'm not sure but I think Magie died. Frank and I are in New York."

"I'm on my way to the animal hospital, Juliette. Have somebody bring the dog over there". Joe replied. Comare called the cops and had an officer help her carry Magie into the car.

Joe called a few minutes later.

"Juliette, I am not exactly sure what happened but I can tell you that the dog had no idea what was going on. He didn't have a heart attack, that's for sure. If he had, his eyes would have been open and his muscles contracted. This dog was dead asleep stretched out all the way when one second, the lights were on and the next, they were off. He never knew what was happening."

Frank had been patiently standing by my side, knowing what was about to come, ready for the onslaught. I hung up the phone and looked up at him, tears streaming down my face. He opened his arms and in I went, crying my heart out.

I was sad. I was very sad. But I immediately thanked God for doing what I had been begging him to do all these years. My little boy died beautifully, painlessly and peacefully. Still, death is tough to take.

Here's the email I sent out a couple of days later:
*In a message dated 02/11/08 07:18:16*
*juliette@centerofthought.com writes:*

*About 12 years ago, I was given a choice between a goldfish and a chow chow. Realizing that goldfish are sucky coddlers, I chose the chow chow. Well actually, my breeders worked a bit differently - they let their chow chows choose the people. A few days after Magie was born, I visited him and his brothers and sisters armed with a worn t-shirt that I had to leave with the litter.*

*Of course, the prettiest of them all chose me and an amazing relationship was born. The first few years, Magie took care of me. His soft, beautiful black coat willingly absorbed many of my tears. In the worst of moments I would look at him and know it would be ok.*

*Later on, I was the only one who figured out how to save his life - over and over again at the total amazement of all vets I had previously consulted. Magie trusted me, I trusted him. When we met Frank and moved to Nahant, life became a dream. The first time he walked into "his" new yard, he ran around and hopped and jumped and sniffed the salty ocean air and felt right at home. (I did the same thing, actually).*

*Then Magie started to get a little old, a bit slow and I swear selectively deaf.... I prayed all the time asking God to never let him suffer and to please, when the time came, to take him quickly and painlessly. My worst fear was to watch this magnificent friend grow really old and sick and then having to put him down.*

*Last Saturday, around 1:00 pm while Frank and I were in New York, lighting a candle at St. Patrick's Cathedral and saying thanks for all the beauty in our life, Magie passed away in his sleep. My babysitter found him "sleeping" next to his favorite chair downstairs, completely stretched out just like he always slept. The vet called me a few minutes later and assured me that it was instantaneous - cardiac arrhythmia or something like it - not even a heart attack - just an immediate, pain free passing on.*

*I got the call around 5 pm. He was fine at Noon - napping in his bed, and by 5 pm rigamortis (sp?) had already set in. That's why I know God granted me my wish while we were in church.*

*Amazingly - miraculously, God also gave me another gift exactly 2 weeks ago. He chose a kitten for us and the circumstances around us getting Moose are too good not to share.* (Which I did).

*Initially, he and Magie were a bit leery of each other - but in 3 days tolerated each other and after 1 week ate and drank out of the same bowl. Then with Magie laying next to me on the couch (where he always was) - Moose jumped*

87

*up and began licking his foot (where he had two toes amputated last year). Magie looked up, and went happily back to sleep in my lap.*

*Magie never ever did anything wrong in his life. My last memory of him is Sat. early morning, jumping around in the snow outside, wagging his tail playing with Frank. He will always be alive for me. Magie died the same way he lived - always protecting me.*

*Yesterday, (we couldn't get out of NY Sat), Frank and I went back to St. Patrick's Cathedral, again to say a prayer of thanks. I had a vision of Magie laying next to Jesus' feet. And why not?*

*Magie was assigned to me to bring love, affection, hope and joy into my life when I needed it the most. Now, I am sure somebody else is in desperate need of his gentle soul. Choose carefully, God, he is very, very special.*

*Juliette*

Love Banghart, Magie's breeder, responded immediately:

*-------- Original Message --------*
*Subject: Re: Good Bye Teddy bear*
*Date: Mon, February 11, 2008 9:33 am*
*To: juliette@centerofthought.com*

*Dearest Juliette and Frank, I am so sad to hear of Magie's passing and am grateful for all that you did for Magie. You were his choice from the beginning...I remember when he chose you to be his personal "human" and then how he carried your t-shirt around and slept on it...even when he was just a tiny tyke, he knew that he was brought on this earth to care for you and be by your side...he was a wonderful boy and you were a wonderful Chow mom.*

*I know that Moose will be a very special companion for you too....especially since Magie and he got to talk and spend time together before Magie left. Chows are very catlike and the two species truly do understand one another.*

*There will never be another Magie, but in time, as you and you family (including Moose) decide to have another Chow baby join your life, I will be happy to help the right little chowlet to find you.*

*You are wonderful and Bob and I thank you for giving Magie the great life that he deserved.*

*Love and Bob*

A few weeks later, a happy, chubby, highly energetic red Chow Chow arrived from Colorado and instantly melted into our hearts and home. He didn't look like a Max. He looked like trouble, big trouble. We had to come up with a name that fit and Wasabi seemed perfect. These animals had no idea how much strength and support they were about to give me.

> "THERE IS SACREDNESS IN TEARS. THEY ARE NOT THE MARK OF WEAKNESS, BUT OF POWER. THEY SPEAK MORE ELOQUENTLY THAN TEN THOUSAND TONGUES. THEY ARE MESSENGERS OF OVER-WHELMING GRIEF... AND OF UNSPEAKABLE LOVE."
>
> **Washington Irving**

# CALLING MOM AND DAD

Thursday, July 10th, 2008

I went to get a facial at Skin for All Seasons in Revere. Linda had been taking care of my skin for 4 years and it needed some attention. She is one of the funniest, giving, spontaneously beautiful people I know. She looked at my skin and asked me if I had been stressed out about something. Even though I knew that I was not supposed to say anything, I just couldn't hold back. I started crying and said:

"Frank has pancreatic cancer, Linda."

She immediately burst into tears herself, then grabbed my hands and asked:

"Can I pray with you, Juliette?" I nodded.

And pray she did. How beautiful is that?

As magical as her hands were, and as relaxing as facials typically are, it didn't work that day. I did feel a little better while I was there, but reality hit again hard as soon as I left.

I went to Whole Foods and walked around like a zombie. I looked at the people in the store and felt like screaming at them "do you have any idea what we are going through?!" Then I wondered how many of the people in here had to cope with their own tragedies. I bought some of the things I was supposed to, but forgot most of them. I felt like an outsider in my own body and nothing seemed real.

Back home, I had to make some calls. Ever since my dad suffered from three heart attacks, I have been very protective of him. He is an extremely sensitive man who, like me, cries at the drop of a hat when things get emotional. He has turned into the most tolerant, loving, supportive and affectionate dad and I admire and love him to pieces. I wanted to call them as their little girl – needing support and strength. Instead, I had to sound positive and strong for them. They didn't take the news well and dad immediately started to cry. My mom kept saying that this was so unfair and how could God allow this to happen. I assured them that we were in the best of hands and that luckily we caught it early. Lucky us indeed...

Mom kept sending us card after card, letter after letter during the coming months. Her words warmed our hearts and encouraged our spirit. She too has turned into the most loving, supportive, affectionate parent in her later years and I love, adore and appreciate everything about her.

# MARIE-LOU, ANGEL NUMBER ONE

I first met Marie-Lou at a women's luncheon in Beverly. Somebody told me that there was another Swiss woman in the room and I was determined to find her. I liked her immediately, but we didn't really have time to talk. A few months went by, and we'd run into each other occasionally – meeting at various holistic health group gatherings – me as a hypnotherapist, she as a life coach. When people ask us how we became such good friends, I always tell them that we were like two dogs sniffing each others' butts for a couple of years, until we finally both decided that we liked what we sniffed. LouLou never much liked that analogy… Time, in our lives, has always been precious and neither one of us wanted to waste it on a relationship that didn't contribute or enhance our life.

I always considered myself a highly evolved human being; that is until Marie- Lou opened her mouth. This lady has an understanding of the human mind and its mechanism, as well as a grasp and understanding of the Divine Connection that continues to render me speechless. Whenever the weather and our time permitted, we'd go for long walks on the beach or in the Lynn Woods, exchanging ideas and healing the world. To this day, I cannot look Marie-Lou in the eyes without tearing up – there's a light that shines so brightly inside of her that just catching a glimpse of its Divine essence takes my breath away. She says that it is my recognition of that light within myself that resonates with such love.

# 5.4%

---

That afternoon, I went online to research pancreatic cancer and my world came crashing down on me. Survival rate: 5.4%. I doubled over at my desk and felt myself being pulled into the fetal position. I couldn't move. I couldn't breathe. I let myself fall to the floor and crawled to the phone, somehow managing to dial my friend, mentor and Angel Number One; Marie-Lou. She picked up the phone but I couldn't make a sound. I tried to talk, but my throat was closed. I tried to breathe, kneeling on the floor in my office and finally, some God forsaken noise came out.

"Juliette?" Marie-Lou asked hesitantly. I have no idea how she knew it was me; we have an unlisted number. I still couldn't talk. I still couldn't breathe.

"Juliette, is that you?"

I knew I had to say something; otherwise she might confuse me with a perverted caller and hang up on me. Somehow, from deep inside, came something that must have sounded like a yes.

"Oh sweetie, are you ok?" she asked.

I still couldn't talk and by now I must have sounded like I was choking and dying.

"JouJou, sit down and breathe. Remember how we worked on breathing? Whatever is going on in your mind right now, shift 50% of your attention away from that and onto your breath. That's good honey, place 50% of your attention on breathing in, feel your breath enter your nose, down your throat and into your lungs, and now 50% of your awareness on your breath as it leaves your body. Good. Now let's continue doing this for a while, ok? You still know and feel everything that's going on around you and within you, but keep 50% of your attention on your breath. Breathing in, breathing out. Breathing in, breathing out. That's it."

LouLou must have talked me into breathing for at least 10 minutes before I could function. When I told her what was going on, she simply said:

"No problem sweetie, we can handle pancreatic cancer. Frank is going to be ok."

"Lou, it says that pancreatic cancer is one of the fastest, deadliest cancers and that some people die within the first few weeks after being diagnosed," I sobbed.

"I don't care what it says, Juliette. Whoever came up with these numbers doesn't know you, and they certainly don't know Frank!"

Gulp.

"So you think there is hope?" I asked.

"Are you kidding me? Oh my God yes! As long as there is life, there is hope. Just look at Paul and how he is feeling these days."

Paul, Marie-Lou's hubby, was diagnosed with Testicular Cancer many years ago and he felt like the chemo was killing him. So he took himself off of all drugs and put himself on a raw food diet. Marie-Lou came flying in from Switzerland to help take care of him and eventually they got married.

"That's true." I said, blowing my nose, "so that's what we'll do. We go raw. When can you come over and teach me all about it?"

"How about Paul and I come over and bring you dinner tonight?" she said, her voice smiling.

They came over with bags full of raw food from Organic Café in Beverly. And even though I was not particularly hungry, I nibbled on a variety of foods I'd never had before. Frank thought the whole thing was just great. We had such an intense time that we almost forgot to go to MGH in Chelsea for Frank's 10:30 pm CT scan.

# A SNOT-DRENCHED KISS

Friday, July 11, 2008

This is the chapter I've been dreading writing about the most. I have a huge knot in my stomach and tears are already streaming down my face and I haven't even started yet. But here I go.

Today we were going to find out about the two spots in Frank's liver. This time, I was in old jeans, a sweatshirt and sneakers; being taken seriously was no longer important.

We understood from Cristina that if the two spots were cancerous, he would not qualify for the Whipple.

"If he doesn't qualify for the Whipple, what are we going to do then?" I asked.

"You could do chemo and hopefully prolong his life a little bit," she said.

"By how long?" I asked.

"Maybe a few weeks," she replied.

"I don't think we'd want to do that – poisoning him and making him suffer much more for just a few more days or weeks."

"I totally agree," Cristina said.

They took Frank back into the prep room while I sat in the waiting room, trying to keep it together. I was nauseous, weak and scared out of my head. This was it. This was going to decide whether Frank would have a chance or not. A while later, a nurse came and brought me to Frank's bed for a last kiss before they wheeled him off into the OR. Dr. Ferrone and her Nurse Practitioner were there, smiling encouragingly at me. I looked at Frank and immediately burst into tears – then I crawled into his bed, wrapped myself in his arms, and held on for dear life, sobbing. Out of the corner of my eyes, I saw Dr. Ferrone's eyes turn red and moist, then she quietly left the room.

"You're so cute. I love you." Frank whispered in my ear, stroking my hair.

When Dr. Ferrone came back a few minutes later, she smiled and said:

"Juliette, this is not a big surgery, this is the easy part."

"I know, but it's so hard being here, three days before our first wedding anniversary, dealing with cancer," I gagged out, tears streaming down my face.

She gave me a look full of sympathy and care, and once again, her eyes got wet. That's when I fell in love with her. I knew right then and there that we had not only a great surgeon, but a warm, caring, compassionate friend in our corner.

They wheeled him off after yet another wet, snot-drenched kiss. I wandered around the hospital, aimlessly, for a few minutes – trying to stay positive. I was texting Joanna, my sister in law whom I adore. I was also texting LouLou, Micki and Moira, and the four of them got me through the longest and worst hour and a half of my life.

All of a sudden, the door to the waiting area flew open and Dr. Ferrone herself came through, looking for me, finding me, giving me the biggest, most beautiful smile I'd ever seen in my life. I knew right then and there that the spots were not cancerous and that Frank would be given a chance at life, even though it was only 5.4%.

That night, at 10 pm, we had to drive to Chelsea again for yet another scan. After Frank went in, I had another full blown panic attack. I ran outside and sat in the car, shaking and howling. Who could I call for support at this time? I dialed Micki's number and hoped that she would answer. Thank God she did. I was literally screaming in pain and Micki, who under normal circumstances would have just told me to shut up already, remained very quiet on the other end, listening. When I finally had to come up for air, she said: "Juliette, I'm here with my sister Terrie. Let's pray, ok?"

"Ok." I don't remember who said what, but I do remember the following words:

"Lord, grant Juliette and Frank the strength, dignity and courage to walk down the path you have chosen for them."

Those words stayed with me and continue to do so every day, no matter what. Micki finished with her favorite prayer:

"Cover you with the blood of Jesus, from the top of your head to the bottom of your feet. Surround you with angels, breathe the Holy Spirit upon you, and let your Guardian Angel lead you."

I was calm now, drying my tears. Then Micki said with total and utter conviction:

"Juliette, Frank is going to be ok. I can feel it. I know it. I don't know how, but I know it. He's going to be fine."

# HOPE, LIFE
# AND A DREAM

Saturday, July 12, 2008

I went through the entire kitchen and got rid of everything that wasn't raw. Then I called to get my prescription of Ambien refilled. Again. I kept accumulating an impressive amount of the little white pills. There were times I was so overwhelmed with fear and desperation that I wanted to give myself a way out, just in case Frank was not going to make it. The idea of living without him was incomprehensible. Going "home" with him seemed like the right thing to do. Bernie picked up on that one day and flat out asked me:

"JouJou, what are you going to do if Frank dies?"

"What do you mean, Bernie?" I played stupid.

"What I mean, is, can you live without him?"

"I don't know, Bernie. I don't know."

"Yeah, that's what I was afraid of," she replied, worried.

That afternoon, a tiny little package arrived from Patty and Dave La Roche, very dear friends of ours and yes, it is THE Dave La Roche who used to pitch for the New York Yankees. We had always joked about renting a pink RV and farting around the country for a year after the guys retired. In the little package, wrapped in pink paper, was a little pink RV along with the most beautiful card. It's impossible to tell you what these little things meant to us and if you know someone who is sick, don't just think about sending cards and little thoughtful gifts – do it. To this day, that little pink RV is sitting on the back of my computer docking station. Once in a while, a patient asks me what it is and why it's there. Usually, I just smile and find a way to avoid an answer. On rare occasions I explain why it represents hope, life, and a dream.

# LAB RAT NUMBER THIRTEEN

Monday, July 14, 2008

Today, on our first wedding anniversary, we once again headed to Mass General and met with Dr. Jill Allen, Oncology, Ted Hong, Radiation Oncology, and their Nurse Practitioner Barbara. It was like visiting a foreign country not understanding the local language. We learned about different Chemotherapies, Proton Beam Radiation, drugs to offset the side effects of drugs and so on. We were also told about a current, ongoing fifteen people study conducted by Mass General on pancreatic cancer.

Frank qualified as lab rat number thirteen. He was to undergo two weeks of oral Capecitabine (Xeloda) Chemotherapy together with 1 week of Proton Beam Radiation, 1 week off, and then the Whipple, followed by six rounds of intravenous Gemsitabine (Gemzar) Chemotherapy. When we asked why the two weeks of oral chemo, they said that it would enhance the radiation. The program was to start on Monday, July 28th.

# TOM TAM, ANGEL
# NUMBER TWO

In the meantime, God sent us Tom Tam, Angel Number Two (I can hear you, Tom, mumbling "whatever," shaking your head…)

When LouLou first told me about Tom back in March, I did some research on the Net and thought she'd totally lost her marbles. *You've got to be kidding me*, I thought. Here's a little Chinese dude, in the midst of a "Guinea Pig Class", banging away on a plastic doll with a little hammer, yelling out letters and numbers. Even more astonishing was that he was surrounded by like-minded idiots banging along with him. This was outrageous! *How dare he take advantage of sick, desperate people and just how much does this schmuck charge for this insanity?* $0.00. *Huh. That's weird.* My assumption of a money-hungry-advantage-taking-snake-oil-salesman was suddenly in doubt.

I read on, watching interviews, listening to stories and testimonies. *Well, maybe if people really want to believe in something like this, it just could help*, I thought, my training as a hypnotherapist agreeing whole heartedly with this placebo-effect assessment.

A few weeks later, I was covered in hives from head to toe. Frank and I, along with Will, Joanna and her husband Rock'n Roll Bob, Moira and some other friends, went to the New Orleans Jazz Festival in early April where I sucked down at least fifty raw oysters, chased by a bucket of Craw Daddies….

I went to the Brigham and Women's Hospital's Division of Rheumatology, Immunology and Allergy, underwent just about every allergy test known to man, all coming up with nothing. I ended up with two prescriptions, neither of them doing anything for me.

*What the hell, what do I have to lose*, I thought, driving to Tom Tam's office located at 85 Essex Street in Haverhill on a sunny Saturday afternoon in early May, looking fabulous, ready to be taken seriously. The area was not exactly what I expected – it looked like an old meat packing district. I finally found the funky, gold-colored number 85, took the elevator to the 2$^{nd}$ floor and found myself in a strange looking hallway. "Doctor's Office" was that last thing to come to mind. I walked down the long corridor, with doors on either side and came to a big, open space. Kitaro, my all time favorite new age musician, was humming softly through the sound system. I filled out an intake form and waited, surprised by the normal looking people in the "office". Finally a door flew open and bonjour, Mr. Voodoo Man himself. I was going to introduce myself when Tom, staring at me, yanked the intake form out of my hands, clearly wondering where this giraffe had come from, and pointed to a room.

"Sit." He continued to stare at me, his fingers "massaging" the air around him. I was just about to explain the reason for my visit, when he said:

"Allergy." He got up and dug his thumb into T4 along my spine. I stoically held back a scream that would have blown Tom right out the window.

"Mpfh! No, actually, I've been tested for all allergies and I don't have allergies." I gasped through clenched teeth, holding back tears.

"ALLERGY!" Tom yelled, continuously banging on a poor little plastic doll with a silver hammer.

"Lay down." He demanded.

Oh boy. Down I went and before I knew it, I had 20 needles in my ankles, knees, back, neck and head. Then I was told to sleep. I couldn't wait to get out of there.

To my utmost joy, I was getting better and better with each treatment, until I finally found out that I was indeed allergic – to the sun! Tom worked on my "amuse", or as you know it, the immune system, and before I knew it, all my hives and some of my doubts were gone. Ergo, schlepping Frank to see Tom seemed like the sensible thing to do.

Tom stared at Frank, dug his thumb into T7 right side of Frank's spine, and for a second I thought Frank was going to beat the shit out of Tom. Instead, his knees buckled and he doubled over.

"Aha!" Tom exclaimed. "Pancri!" Pancri means pancreas.

Frank was shown into room number two and was asked to sit down on the bed. Tom sat across from him, concentrating, while I was smiling quietly in the corner. Tom started "massaging" the air, quite obviously not interested in a single word Frank had to say. Frank looked more and more miserable by the second.

"How you feel?" Tom asked.

"What?" Frank replied.

"How you feel?" Tom asked again. "You feel warm?"

"Uh, yes, actually, I do," Frank admitted, mildly surprised, casting a sideways glance in my direction.

"Good. Now you lay down." Frank was nose down on the bed and in less than thirty seconds, Tom had twenty needles in his ankles, legs, back, neck and head.

"Sleep!" Tom commanded and walked out the door.

"Honey, you have some 'splaining to do," Frank mumbled into the paper sheet, just before he started snoring. He woke up to Peggy doing Tui Na on him – a spinal massage to unblock the actual, physical knots along the spine. She worked hard on T7. [All of Tom's people are amazing; Monica, Brian, Chucky and Laura– thank you so much!]

LouLou was thrilled that Frank was seeing Tom and immediately signed up for a Tong Ren for Cancer Certification Class. Then she spent half a day explaining to me how to tap for Frank. I started tapping for Frank every day.

# TONG REN

---

Tom Tam: *"The Tong Ren healing system is a modern version of the old system called Huatuojiaji. Doctor Jua Tuo was a famous Chinese Medical doctor born two thousand years ago. Because of politics, Dr. Jua Tuo was killed, his books burned and lost from history. In my practice, I have tried to bring his system back."*

*"The other basis of Tong Ren Healing comes from the Swiss Psychiatrist Carl Jung's theory termed "archetypal formation". These energetic patterns are innately wired into a universal mind or what Jung termed the "Collective Unconscious".*

In the book "Walking out of the Medical Jungle", page 4, Dr. William C. Daly, M.D. writes:

*"Tong Ren Therapy frequently brings hope to people who have received such a diagnosis as cancer. It brings us into connection with others who are ill and many who have been healed. But even more importantly, it brings us into connection with the human collective unconscious, a vast and powerful source of*

*healing energy. Tong Ren empowers us with techniques that are easy to learn, inexpensive, and becoming widely available. And it offers real hope of healing, of improving both quality of life and longevity. Tong Ren practitioners donate their time and energy to guide healing classes (known as guinea pig classes), inviting others into harmonious connection with the collective healing energy. They share the peaceful use of power for healing purposes only, and enjoy the happiness of helping others make dramatic improvements in their lives."*

Tom also indicates the importance of brainwave entrainment. *"If you watch a school of fish in the ocean, they all move as one unit. It's not like the boss fish holds up an arrow that says: "ok dudes, in 3.14 seconds we're all going to go that way." They communicate via brain wave entrainment and if a sardine can do this, what is the human ability?*

According to Dr. Shaw Sprague: *"The theory is based on the notion that the mind has a quantum expression to it which sends and receives signals much like a radio station. When enough people begin to send out a signal, the signal becomes stronger. Tong Ren applies analytical psychology's notion that the collective unconscious is the most powerful force in the universe and uses this cosmic energy to alter physical and non-physical reality."*

*Tom Tam: "In my healing system there are energy loops with three components. The brain, the nervous system and the organs. All energy is conducted from the brain, as the brain is the central computer system within the body. When this computer system has blockages, it can result in erroneous biosignal changes."*

*"There are many ways to heal cancer. When you search for healing cancer on the Internet, you will find many ways and systems. Each healing system fights and denies the others. Tong Ren healing never fights or denies others because we believe in scientific evolution and natural selection." And "We are interested in healing the disease in a scientific way. We are not interested in the hysterical so-called criticism. There is no honor and glory in practicing Tong Ren healing,*

*yet when we heal some cases, especially the "incurable" ones, we feel good in our hearts."*

Dr. William C. Daly, M.D. wrote this for patients to give to their doctors:

*Dear Doctor,*

*Your patient trusts your opinion, and appreciates the care you are providing. Concerned about the gravity of the illness they are facing, your patient is weighing the risks and benefits of all traditional and complementary modalities. They will appreciate your tolerance of their personal choice to add a harmless, noninvasive and inexpensive augmentation to your prescribed treatment.*

*We physicians agree that any good scientist considers all possibilities, unblinded by prejudice or preconception. We acknowledge that Western medicine is imperfect, as we have numerous "incurable" illnesses. There is a Complementary therapy called Tong Ren that can augment healing, but does not replace or delay conventional treatment. It is a combination of Western medical science with Eastern insights, and offers a new approach to treating many terminal illnesses and some debilitating diseases. It introduces the concepts of bioelectricity and of synchronicity with the body's natural health, and also emphasizes the need for stress reduction. Note that Tong Ren practitioners do not practice medicine; they do not diagnose, prescribe, or interfere with traditional medical advice. Most have been healed themselves, or have healed loved ones with this modality.*

*We are documenting scientific evidence that Tong Ren has improved or healed some previously "incurable" conditions, such as refractory cancers, autoimmune diseases and neurologic conditions including amyotrophic lateral sclerosis. There are already thousands of anecdotal reports of such improvements, including my own mother's 'untreatable' metastatic cancer. Others have produced laboratory models and replicable data toward a scientific understanding of energy healing. Please read the following Overview of Tong Ren Healing.*

# OVERVIEW OF TONG REN HEALING

http://tomtam.com/files/tong_ren_overview_dear_doctor.pdf

*Tong Ren is a highly targeted method of directing healing energy to the body. It can achieve extraordinary results by combining complementary elements of Western and Eastern medicine, and is spreading rapidly throughout the world. Its popularity is driven by success at healing or controlling cancers and other debilitating conditions that have not responded to traditional Western medicine or Eastern therapies.*

*Western medical science has developed sophisticated understandings of anatomy, physiology, neurology, biochemistry and cell function. We understand that the health of each organ in the body requires a supply of nutrients, which are mostly transported by blood circulation. Many organs require hormonal stimulation to function normally, and other organs become diseased if they stop receiving ongoing electrical and chemical stimulation via the nervous system. We cannot see any of these functions with the naked eye, so in recent years Western science has developed tools to estimate some of these mechanisms. But no one understands the cause of many serious illnesses, including most cancers, degenerative diseases and autoimmune diseases. And most of these have no cure.*

*Eastern medicine understands that the body requires a continuous supply of an additional form of energy to remain healthy. Each organ needs a natural flow of electrical signals, and blockage of that necessary bioelectric impulse leads to disease. We have not yet developed tools to measure this energy, but many people are able to feel its effects and studies are beginning to show its healing power.*

*East and West have contradictory but complementary understandings of the body, of the mind and of healing. Neither approach is adequate alone, as evidenced by many incurable diseases. Both are necessary components of a healing system to treat all aspects of the whole person, and allow the body to heal or cure those same illnesses. Tong Ren incorporates Western science with Eastern*

116

*wisdom, but is not simply the sum of two sciences. Its healing power grows a quantum leap by harnessing another natural tendency we have all observed in nature: Synchronicity. The animal kingdom demonstrates a capacity we share. The perfectly synchronized movements of birds flying in a flock, or fish swimming in a school are not coordinated by the usual senses of sight, sound, smell, feel or taste -- but rather by "brainwave entrainment" with an instinctive commonality. They move in perfect harmony because each is connected with the brainwave energy and patterns of the group. A natural propensity toward synchronization is even seen in non-biologic systems, such as two pendulum clocks side-by-side on a wall gradually moving into harmony. The human brain has a Frequency Following Response, tending to change its dominant electroencephalogram patterns toward the frequency of external stimuli. Several studies have demonstrated a strong tendency for brainwaves of meditating people to synchronize with each other, with no sensory contact.*

*Dr. Carl Jung, Pierre Teilhard de Chardin, Ervin Laszlo, Gary Zukav and others have described the evolving development of a subconscious human connectedness, like a global spirit or brain. As an anthropologist, Teilhard traced the natural evolution of life on earth from the development of cells, then plants, through animal and finally human form. This visible biologic evolution then progressed to internal intellectual development and now finally to globally evolving organization on the level of spirit-energy. We are all part of this upward spiral of organization, regardless of our awareness. In Tong Ren Therapy we tap into this vast reserve of healthy bioelectrical patterns and health-sustaining energy. We then use the natural tendency toward synchronicity to bring diseased organs back into harmony with the healthy bioelectric patterns of Tong Ren practitioners, and even more importantly into entrainment with the more powerful global brain.*

*Eastern medicine understands that the body has a natural tendency to heal, but requires the normal supply of nutrients and stimuli noted above. This suggests that many cancers and other debilitating illnesses occur because a blockage prevents flow of health-sustaining bioelectric signals. Tong Ren practitioners work to remove these blockages, and restore the normal flow of nurturing and healing energy. They use an acupuncture figurine as a tool. They apply energy to particular points on this anatomic model with a lightweight magnetic hammer or other methods, focusing their conscious mind on locations corresponding to the patient's blockages. Their rhythmic and habitual tapping produces a connection between the subconscious of the practitioner and the corresponding locations on the patient's body to open the blockages. This subconscious connection creates a conduit, drawing the diseased organ back into entrainment with the healthy bioelectrical signals and vast healing energy of the global collective unconscious. Health is usually restored, if the conscious mind does not reject or block the process. The identity of the individual practitioner is immaterial, because the healing power does not come from that practitioner, but rather from the collectively evolving milieu.*

*Imagine the Tong Ren practitioner as a piano tuner. The tuner's hammer strikes piano wires of errant pitch, so they may be adjusted back into harmony with the healthy collective frequencies. The actual retensioning of the cords is accomplished <u>not</u> by the individual tapper, but by the energy in an unseen chorus of experts. The accepting recipient feels energetic change, and then the medical tests usually improve. Most Tong Ren practitioners have themselves been healed, or have healed loved ones in this manner. Such healing is a powerful yet humbling experience. Practitioners happily welcome people with illnesses incurable by traditional Western or Eastern medicine. They simply act as a conduit for the healing frequencies and power of the Collective. They are rewarded by the joy and comfort of the healed.*

*Energy healing is most effective if we are receptive and accepting of that energy on a core level. Many people desperately want to heal but are not able to relax into such acceptance, because it lies outside of their understanding of reality. Preconceptions may prevent them from benefiting from any form of energy healing, but if we can help them "see" beyond their five senses, they may be able to open their hearts and accept healing energy. Many ancient cultures had that insight, and some contemporary scientists and philosophers are working toward that vision.*

*Throughout human history "everyone knew" that the sun and stars revolved around the earth -- until about 400 years ago, when we developed tools to see beyond our assumptions. We can never see gravity, other forms of energy or other levels of reality, but we can certainly measure their effects. Discoveries in quantum mechanics and particle physics indicate that the reality we experience in three-dimensional space and time is only one relatively small and transient domain of reality. There are other aspects of reality which we cannot see with our five senses, and these domains underlie and interact with the realm we experience. In this new vision of multiple interconnected domains of reality, our cognitive and spiritual energies interact with an underlying universal energy field, which is inherently organized and naturally healthy. Illness occurs when our body becomes uncoupled or "blocked" from these deeper levels of reality. There is a fundamental coherence in the universe that is enduring in time which we experience as synchronicity. If we provide a conduit for our manifest reality to reconnect and re-synchronize with the original underlying but unob-servable energies and domains of reality, we then bring our three-dimensional space-time "diseased reality" back into harmony with original natural "healthy reality". Physicist Dr. William Tiller and others have produced models and replicable scientific evidence that we can, in fact, change our physical reality through human intention to invoke such coherence.[1] Ervin Laszlo adds histori-cal and global insights into improving ourselves and our world through simi-larly enhanced understanding and vision of reality.*

*The practice of Tong Ren is spreading rapidly, and it is now available in at least 24 of the United States, and at least 15 countries. A medical study was pub-lished in 2008, evaluating the effect of Tong Ren on 265 patients at 7 different sites in Massachusetts and Connecticut with cancer, autoimmune, endocrine, musculoskeletal and other disorders. 89% of patients responded positively to the Tong Ren Therapy, including healing of numerous cancers and other serious illnesses. Please take a moment to review The Tong Ren Healing Method: A Survey Study – AM Sullivan, S Bauer-Wu, M Miovic - Complementary Health Practice Review, 2008,*

*http://chp.sagepub.com/cgi/content/abstract/14/1/19.    Traditional    Western medicine physicians and researchers are demonstrating increasing interest in Tong Ren, and Healing Classes are now being held in some traditional Western medical facilities. Scientific studies to demonstrate the effectiveness of Tong Ren are in development.*

*TCM practitioner Tom Tam has been developing Tong Ren Healing for more than 25 years, and he continues its evolution. Tom is a healer, acupuncturist, Chi Gong and Tai Chi expert, writer and poet living in Boston, Massachusetts. Tom has used Tong Ren to heal thousands of patients, and has trained hundreds of practitioners who share this healing method around the world. Tong Ren is a Complementary therapy, rather than an alternative to traditional medical care. Tong Ren practitioners depend on the patient's physician to diagnose the cause of an illness. They do not practice medicine; they do not diagnose, prescribe, interfere with traditional medical advice, or promise a cure. They DO invite each patient to synchrony with healthy universal energy, and thereby restore health by healing or stabilizing an ailment. Tong Ren Therapy opens new horizons for medical professionals and other healers, and for anyone hoping to return to health.*

For those of you familiar or interested in Tong Ren Therapy, I open the Sky Window, then go to GV20 (Association Cortex), GV22 (Human Growth Hormone), BL6 (Pituitary), TW17 (Human Growth Hormone Releasing Hormone / Metabolism, GB13, GV17, BL9, St. 10 - LI17 – GB12(Phrenic Nerve), Satellite Cells to the Vegus Nerve, Glial Cells, Splanchnic nerves to enteric nervous system T5 – L5 and the Immune System, T1,2,3,4,7, focusing mostly on T7, continuing to T8,9,10,11,12, then open the kidney meridians, St. 21., 25, 36, grounding to L3 and K1.

When I work with clients, I also pray for them.  However, it is important to know that <u>Tong Ren is not a religion or based on any religious influence. It is strictly science.</u>

To learn more about Tong Ren, go to <u>www.TomTam.com</u>

# HONEY, WHAT'S WRONG?

---

I was finally doing **something**. For the past few weeks I had been useless, drowning in shock and panic, while Frank level-headedly continued working. I couldn't focus or concentrate on anything. I couldn't read, I couldn't

123

watch television, I couldn't even play hearts on the computer. The only thing I could think of was crocheting and I don't crochet. Ever. But here I was, beginning what was going to be a simple little blanket. Piece by piece it came together while I worked at it at home and at the hospital until a few months later, it ended up being the size of a small European country. It now covers our king sized bed, dangling from all sides, and the humongous purple cross in the middle keeps us warm and protected.

The other thing I did was record an Immune System Strengthening CD for Frank. Understanding the powerful results that can come from hypnotism, I poured my heart and soul into the work. [Now, whenever I work with a client who suffers from a serious illness or disease, I remember exactly where I was back then and this allows me to relate on a much deeper, personal level].

Just when I thought I could handle things, I started to PMS and gone was my new found courage. I was sobbing all day, wallowing in misery, self-pity and despair. Poor Moose ran whenever he saw me coming; he was desperate to protect his fur from the constant onslaught of my snot and tears.

I was able to pull myself together again when Frank came home, only to fall apart immediately once we got into bed.

"Honey, what's wrong?" Frank asked.

"Nothing." I said.

I never told Frank about his 5.4% chance of survival and I was not about to tell him then, either.

"U huh. Come here." Frank gathered me into his arms. "Sweetie, tell me what's going on."

"YOU HAVE A 5.4% SURVIVAL RATE," I blurted out before I started balling hysterically.

"Really? That's not so good." Frank laughed.

I looked up at him, a mixture of tears and snot dripping onto his left shoulder. *He must be in a state of total shock,* I thought.

"I can't believe you're laughing. Are you ok?" I asked.

"Yeah, I'm ok." He said, smiling.

"How can you be ok? This is not ok. I can't even think of losing you. I can't live without you." I sobbed.

"You're not going to lose me sweetheart. I'm going to be one of those 5.4%, that's all," he said matter of factly.

"You are?"

"Without a doubt. Unquestionably. If there are other people that survive this thing, so will I. This is just one more battle, no big deal," he declared, handing me a Kleenex, taking off his shirt carefully avoiding touching the left shoulder.

I thought about Frank's battles and was suddenly convinced that he was right. He had to be.

Since there was no doubt in Frank's mind that he would be one of the 5.4%, I didn't want there to be any doubt in mine, either. I snuggled in and we began one of my favorite good-night rituals.

"Do you love me?" I asked.

"More than anything!" He answered, promptly.

"How much?" I wanted to know.

"Oh, more than the total amount of any hair that has ever been on any animal, since the beginning of time, to all eternity!" he responded.

"What about people's hair?" I asked.

"And all the hairs of all the people that have ever lived and ever will live," he replied.

"What about scales?"

"Ah, of course. I love you more than any hair on any creature there ever was and ever will be, and all the scales of all the creatures that have ever lived and ever will live."

"Feathers?" I had to know.

"How silly of me! Yes, more than all the hairs and all the scales and all the feathers that ever were and ever will be on this planet."

"What about the other planets?" I continued probing.

"And all the planets we know!" he exclaimed.

"What about planets we don't know?"

"Absolutely. And all the planets we've never even heard of, too!"

"What about all the planets in all the other galaxies?"

"I love you more than the combined total of all hairs, scales, feathers of all creatures that ever were and ever will be, on all planets known and unknown, in all galaxies, including all heavenly objects and all stars!"

"Wow. That's a lot of love!" I said, beaming.

"And that's not even half of it, sweetheart."

# TREATMENT OUTLINE

---

July 16th, 2008

To make this book as real and as personal as possible, I have decided to copy my actual emails from that time. Each one is an invitation to you to share that time of our life in the most intimate way.

-------- *Original Message* --------
*Subject: Update on The Frank!*
*From: juliette@centerofthought.com*
*Date: Wed, July 16, 2008 6:19 pm*
*To: Family*

*We met with the surgeon (Cristina Ferrone) this morning. Here's the detailed outline:*

*July 28th:    1 Week of Proton Beam Radiation w/ low dose Chemo (pill form)*

*August 4th:  1 Week of continued low dose Chemo (pill form)*

*August 11th: 1 Week Off*

*August 18th: 7:00 a.m. Whipple Surgery, In hospital for approximately 7 Days*

*September:   Recovery at Home*

*October - March: Chemo (3 weeks on, 1 week off, etc.)*

*Frank and I went for a 3 hour hike today and feel great!  We are in the BEST hands - (I'm in love with Dr. Cristina Ferrone!!!!!!).*

*We have reduced our "100% Raw Food Diet" to about 60% - Frank was losing weight and that's the last thing he needs right now - so tonight: I'm making Cheeseburgers!!!!!!!!!!!!!!!*

*In the mornings, we have fresh fruit smoothies, and homemade raw & organic granola.  Lunch will be "normal" - some form of protein and veggies - dinners start with a raw organic veggie smoothie and then something light (buckwheat, asparagus, egg omelet, etc..  Frank actually feels better right now than he has in MONTHS - and we are really grateful to be able to take part in this medical protocol.*

*I haven't cried in two full days!!!!!!!!!!!!!!!!!!!!!! and feel absolutely confident that Frank will pull through this SHINING AND BETTER THAN EVER.  There are several people that had the Whipple due to pancreatic "problems" and a bunch of them have lived for 10+ years free of cancer.*

*Oh - Dr. Ferrone will have a pathologist in the O.R. with her - so when she cuts "stuff" out, he'll look at it to determine whether the "edges" / lymph nodes contain any cancerous cells and if they do, she'll just cut a bit more until they get it all!  (that's not to say that there might not be any microscopic cancer cells left, but we'll nuke those bastards with the chemo).*

*That's all for now. We are praying (lots), do some acupuncture and energy healing, hypnotherapy, meditation, eating right - everything we can. I am absolutely confident this is going to turn out great!*

*Love, JouJou*

July 25th, 2008

-------- *Original Message* --------
*Subject: Update*
*From: juliette@centerofthought.com*
*Date: Fri, July 25, 2008 10:57 am*
*To: Family and Friends*

*I've been asked by some people to send out status reports as to what's happening as far as Frank's trip to recovery is concerned. Everyone on this list is close to our hearts and is asked to keep any and all information confidential.*

*We just got confirmation that everything is on schedule for next Monday. Proton Beam Radiation and oral Chemo start Monday at 12:00 Noon, Proton goes through Friday. Keep your positive thoughts and prayers coming; they're working!!!*

*Until next week, with warm regards,*

*Juliette*

"CAPECITABINE (XELODA) *IS A NEW ORAL DRUG. TECHNICALLY, IT IS CLASSIFIED AS A TUMOR-ACTIVATED FLUOROPYRIMIDINE CARBAMATE, SIMILAR TO THE DRUG FLUOROURACIL (5-FU). A LARGE MULTICENTER PHASE II TRIAL TESTED THE EFFICACY AND SAFETY OF ORAL CAPECITABINE TAKEN TWICE PER DAY. THE TRIAL WAS CENTERED AT BAYLOR UNIVERSITY MEDICAL CENTER, IN DALLAS. A TOTAL OF 163 PATIENTS WERE ENTERED INTO THIS STUDY AT 25 CENTERS, AND ALL BUT ONE RECEIVED CAPECITABINE.*

*THE OVERALL RESPONSE RATE WAS 20 PERCENT WITH 3 COMPLETE RESPONSES. ALL RESPONDING PATIENTS WERE RESISTANT TO OR HAD FAILED PACLITAXEL, AND ALL HAD RECEIVED AN ANTHRACYCLINE-TYPE DRUG. THE MEDIAN TIME TO DISEASE PROGRESSION WAS 93 DAYS, THE DURATION OF RESPONSE WAS 8.1 MONTHS, AND THE OVERALL SURVIVAL TIME WAS 12.8 MONTHS.*

*SIDE EFFECTS INCLUDED PAIN AND DISCOMFORT IN THE HANDS AND FEET, DIARRHEA, NAUSEA, VOMITING AND FATIGUE. DIARRHEA AND HAND AND FOOT SYMPTOMS OCCURRED WITH SEVERE INTENSITY IN MORE THAN 10 PERCENT OF PATIENTS [J CLIN ONCOL 1999;17:485].*"

**Ralph W. Moss, PH.D.**
**Questioning Chemotherapy**

# CAPECITABINE (XELODA)

Monday, July 28, 2008

Frank took his first Xeloda oral chemo pill and off we were to his first proton beam radiation treatment. I asked him if he felt anything from the pill. "Not really, maybe a bit of a rush, that's all."

We got to Mass General's Jackson Building, Room 121, and easily found the waiting area. I was horrified by the amount of kids that were in the room. Some in wheelchairs, others on crutches – most of them horrendously skinny and bald. I searched out the faces of the mothers, astonished by the strength I saw in them. These were just kids, some of them really little. They haven't even begun to live life. I felt sick.

Frank was called and the previously tattooed spots on his stomach were targeted by the proton laser beam. After the treatment, the radiologist walked up to me and asked me if I wanted to see the laser while Frank was getting dressed. Absolutely.

At approximately three stories high, this "thing" was humongous. *All that for a tiny beam of light*, I thought.

Every day that week we drove to Mass General for Frank's treatments. It went well; no side effects. Even the sight of all those kids started to look familiar. We saw Tom on Thursday and Saturday, hoping he could do his "magic" to offset the radiation damage, which could leave scar tissues, resulting in slowing down the healing process.

Frank took a steam shower every single day, sometimes twice a day, in order to sweat out the poisons and toxins from the chemo and the radiation. We added essential oils such as Eucalyptus, which is anti-inflammatory, antispasmodic, decongestant, deodorant, antiseptic and antibacterial. Rosewood, which is analgesic, anti depressant, anti septic, aphrodisiac, anti bacterial and cephalic. Red Thyme, which is a anti-bacterial and immune boosting, and White Camphor, which is anti-inflammatory and reduces joint and muscle pain. This felt really good to him and he sailed through the week.

# SO I HAVE A WEIRD SENSE OF HUMOR!

---

July 29th, 2008

-----*Original Message*-----
*From: juliette@centerofthought.com*
*Sent: Tuesday, July 29, 2008 7:17 PM*
*To: Family and Friends*
*Subject: Update*

*Hi everyone,*

*Frank's fine. I, on the other hand, had a rather traumatic experience yesterday. I was dicing an onion and almost chopped off a part of my nail! It didn't break, mind you, but I can feel a little rough spot when I touch the side with my left index finger. After Frank held me for a while, assuring me that everything would be ok, I was able to put myself into a deep hypnotic state which enabled me to "let it go" and to "leave the past behind where it belongs". Then I cowgirled up and got busy scheduling an emergency manicure. I feel much better now, having this dark moment behind me.*

*Love,*

*Juliette*

*PS: Did I mention Frank's doing great?*

*Friday, August 1st, 2008*

*From: juliette@centerofthought.com*
*Sent: Friday, August 01, 2008 10:13*
*To: Family and Friends*
*Subject: Update*

*Hello,*

*Well, the first week is almost behind us! Frank has done astonishingly well!!! No nausea, no pain, no broken nails. As a matter of fact, Frank is feeling so good he's recommending this protocol to all of you!*

*Some facts you might find interesting:*

*There are three levels of chemo. Low, Medium and Hard. Hard chemo is for treating leukemia and other "body-cancers" which result in significant side affects (vomiting, hair loss, fatigue, etc). The Medium one is for breast cancer (etc) and also has known side affects. The low dose (Capecitabine or Zeloda) is in pill form and shows no significant side effects (some people - not Frank - can get a bit nauseous but that's all).*

*The proton beam radiation delivers the same amount of radiation in 5 days as typical radiation does in 6 weeks! Because it is so targeted, the body can deal with this huge amount since no other organs are negatively affected.*

*Frank is number 13 out of a 15 person study protocol, and their most spectacular specimen of a lab rat version! Number 14 has just signed on and we are going to try to get in touch with the other "rats" to compare notes on the various modalities they're all experiencing.*

*Speaking of modalities, I am schlepping Frank to all kinds of complementary medical treatments. There's Acupuncture, Tong Ren, Tui Na, Chi Gong, Hypnotherapy and healthy nutrition - except for this week. When you have proton beam therapy, you can not eat anything healthy!!!! Yup, no fruits, no veggies, no raw foods - so we've been literally drowning ourselves in pasta, white bread and mashed potatoes...... Frank looks amazing, holding his weight beautifully, while I, the sympathetic idiot who goes along with everything, is rapidly becoming a tank. Yeah me - that'll be another "Poor Me Email" to come.*

*Keep all your funny, encouraging and loving emails coming - I can't respond to all of them but we keep them so that a few months from now, we can watch the sunset, have a glass of wine and read them all, remembering a chapter in our live that taught us more than anything we could have ever expected.*

*Love, Juliette & Frank*

August 6th, 2008

*From: juliette@centerofthought.com*
*Sent: Wednesday, August 06, 2008 9:40 AM*
*To: Family and Friends*

*Ladies and Gent's,*

*I've been asked by several of you as to what's going on.*

*Well, I had a manicure and feel much better again.*

*Frank is on his second week of chemo and continues to do great. He is working this week and does come home exhausted at night - which is to be fully expected. I immediately throw him into the Steam shower with some essential eucalyptus oil, which is highly detoxifying (in an attempt to get rid of the buzillion of dead cells in his body). Also, we are working hard, in addition to everything else, on getting his body into an alkaline state. Apparently, cancer cells blossom in an acidic environment, but become dormant at an alkaline level of 7.4, and die at 8.4. Frank got up to a 7 this morning and that's after only one day of not eating anything containing yeast, white flour, nothing fermented nor any form of sugar. Oh, and no coffee (which is the worst, by the way).*

*We continue our quest of knowledge and learn more about the body than we'd ever thought possible. I always rather arrogantly assumed that I knew a lot...... yeah, sure, right!*

*Frank will continue to work until Wed. next week, then take Thursday and Friday off so that we can wrap our noodles around the surgery in a rested, positive, even excited way.*

*Thank you all so much for your calls, emails, cards and prayers. Speaking of how great you all are, Frank and I have decided that "all y'all" (that one's for you Patty & Dave!) belong into the Guidara Hall of Friends!*

*Love you all!*

# POTENTIALLY DEADLY ASSUMPTION

Sunday, August 10th, 2008

Frank couldn't get out of bed. He was shaking, shivering and freezing, only to be followed by the worst sweat and heat attacks a few minutes later. We couldn't figure out what was going on and I was scared stiff. *This must be the damn chemo,* I assumed. *This is killing him!* I had read that chemo was only effective in less than 10% of all patients, and was generally doing a lot more damage than good. I hated chemo and what it was doing to my love. Harvey, our dear friend and mountainous teddy bear of a man, showed up that afternoon with a big bag of deli sandwiches and a barrel of laughs. How I needed that! However, after he saw how his buddy was doing, the laughter subsided and harvey drove home, I assume sad and scared.

"AS A CHEMIST TRAINED TO INTERPRET DATA, IT IS INCOM-PREHENSIBLE TO ME THAT PHYSICIANS CAN IGNORE THE CLEAR EVIDENCE THAT CHEMOTHERAPY DOES MUCH, MUCH MORE HARM THAN GOOD."

Alan C. Nixon, Ph.D., Past President, American Chemical Society. From the Article: Chemotherapy: Snake-Oil Remedy, published in the Los Angeles Times, January 9, 1987

Monday, August 11th, 2008

The chills and the fever escalated and Frank turned yellow again. This was something else! We ran to Mass General and after some tests, found out that the stent was displaced and that the bile was backing up into his system again. He could have gone into toxic shock and died at any time. He was wheeled into emergency surgery and Dr. Brenna Bounds removed the old stent and replaced it with a new one. Things eased up again that night, thank God and this team of experts.

I recorded a Pre-Surgery Hypnotherapy CD for Frank which he listened to every night this week. It seemed to help a lot.

> "TO BELIEVE IN GOD FOR ME IS TO FEEL THAT THERE IS A GOD, NOT A DEAD ONE, OR A STUFFED ONE, BUT A LIVING ONE, WHO WITH IRRESISTIBLE FORCE URGES US TOWARDS MORE LOVING."
>
> Vincent van Gogh

# FRANK BECOMES A CHRISTIAN

Wednesday, August 13th, 2008

As a Christian, I have always believed in, and witnessed the power of prayer. I knew instinctively that I had to schedule a prayer conference call, inviting all of our families and friends. Micki allowed me to use her bridge number and the call was held today at 2:00 pm. Frank was upstairs sleeping peacefully. When I tell you that this conference call was powerful, believe me. My parents and sisters called in from Switzerland, Will from New York, Ed from Palm Springs, Micki from Ft. Lauderdale, Moira from Baltimore, Patty and Dave from Fort Scott and Blake from LA. Others were more local in the New England area. I recorded the call onto a CD and I have to be honest, I have not listened to it since. It is so gut-wrenchingly beautiful, emotional and loving that I just can't handle it yet. We all prayed individually for Frank, bombarding God and the heavens with such force and passion that I'm sure God had to sit down. At the end of the call, we ended with "Our Heavenly Father." You cannot even begin to imagine the calls and emails I received afterwards. Some people had never been exposed to the power of prayer, nor to the amount of love that brought us all together. I was doing surprisingly well until the very end, when I totally lost it.

I went up to bed that night and told Frank about it. I also asked him if he wanted to hear it. "Absolutely, I'd love to."

When it was over, Frank was crying. I'd only once seen him cry once before, after his twenty five year old niece died of Leukemia.

We held each other and I silently thanked God for being God, for being so powerful and for our family and friends.

I suddenly woke up in the middle of the night with what I can only describe as a divine epiphany. I woke Frank up and said:

"I know why you got this cancer. God wants you on his team. This is exactly why this is happening." Frank pondered the thought and admitted that it made sense.

"Frank, you have to become a Christian. Right now. I know that that's what God wants, I feel it in every cell in my body."

"You know, I think you're right. What do I do?" I blinked and closed my eyes. I don't even come close to remembering what I said next, firmly believing that the Holy Spirit took over, but it was something like this:

"Repeat after me: I acknowledge Jesus Christ as the Son of God. I acknowledge that He died on the cross for me to take away my sins and to grant me everlasting life. I give my life, my soul, my eternity to you Lord."

# VISIT FROM WILL

Thursday, August 14th, 2008

We were thrilled. Will was coming to visit and Frank was really excited to see his son. We spent lots of time playing games, laughing, walking and talking. We kept everything light – We both felt an overwhelming need to protect Will and didn't want him to know the severity of his Dad's condition.

# PREPARING FOR
# SURGERY

Friday, August 15th, 2008

*From: juliette@centerofthought.com*
*Subject: Update*
*To: Family and Friends*
*Sent: Friday, August 15, 2008, 11:24 AM*

*Hello,*

*Well, it's just about time! Frank and I are spending these days relaxing by the ocean - nice! We apologize to all of you for not returning calls, please understand that it's important for Frank to just "unhook" from the world.*

*Frank had to spend a couple of days in the hospital this week, due to an infection caused by the blocked bile duct stent. After receiving gallons and gallons of intravenous antibiotics, he's doing great again.*

*The surgery is on! We'll check into the hospital Monday morning at 6:30 a.m., the surgery is scheduled for 8:30 a.m. (isn't it amazing that it only takes a couple of hours to prep for such a procedure?!). I will send out a quick blast*

*Monday evening to let you know how well everything went. Frank is mentally already beyond the surgery and the recovery, impatiently waiting to tackle all kinds of action packed days!*

*Will is arriving tomorrow and we plan on having a fun, relaxing weekend together. Games (of course I'll win all of them - right, Will?......) and lots of laughter and well, knowing Frank, healthy competition (meaning he'll kick our asses up, down and sideways).*

*Have a wonderful weekend and keep those prayers going for him.*

*Love Always,*

*Juliette*

# MAKING LOVE FOR THE LAST TIME?

---

Sunday, August 17th, 2008

Making love that night, not knowing whether it would be for the last time, was an experience emotionally and physically so overwhelming I'm not sure I know how to describe it. I could feel every kiss in my hurting heart. Each caress brought forth a never ending stream of tears. With every gently whispered word I fell more and more apart. Would I ever feel Frank's passion again? Would we ever kiss like this again? Would we ever feel each other in love again? I hung on for dear life, sobbing, praying for time to stop. It didn't.

# THE WHIPPLE

Monday, August 18th, 2008

**Before Whipple**

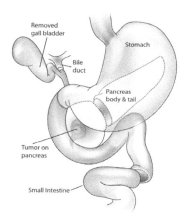

- Removed gall bladder
- Stomach
- Bile duct
- Pancreas body & tail
- Tumor on pancreas
- Small Intestine

**After Whipple**

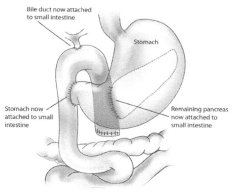

- Bile duct now attached to small intestine
- Stomach
- Stomach now attached to small intestine
- Remaining pancreas now attached to small intestine

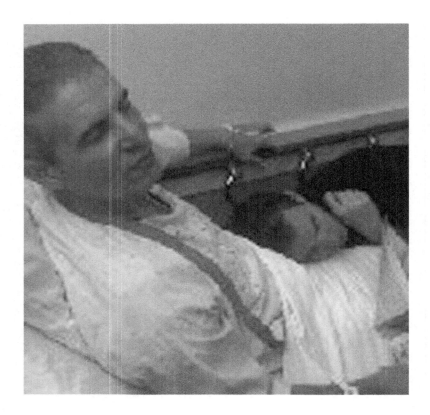

Will is cuddling up just before Frank goes in for the Whipple

Whipple, here we come. We got to the Wang Building at 6:00 am, armed with lip balm and tissues. Joanna was waiting there for us. Dr. Ferrone met with us prior to the surgery, reassuring us once again that she didn't anticipate any problems, and that the surgery should last somewhere around 6 hours. Will was laying in Frank's arms prior to them wheeling him out, Joanna to his right, me faking a smile somewhere to his left.

We were ready for a long day. The waiting area was nice and comfortable and when we thought we were halfway through, the phone rang and I was asked to take the call in a little office. *Oh no. God no. Something's wrong.*

148

"Juliette? It's Cristina. Everything went incredibly well and we're all done! He's being stitched up right now and I should be out in a few minutes to tell you all about it."

I flew back into the waiting area, knowing Joanna and Will were worried sick. "It's over and it went great," I yelled not even halfway back to the table. The relief on their faces mirrored my own as we all got up and hugged ourselves silly.

A short while later, Cristina came in, smiling, and brought us all into a conference room. "So, this was the easiest Whipple I've ever done. First of all, I was amazed at how easily the tumor came out – it almost fell into my hands. The tumor, which was originally the size of an apricot, came out the size of a grape." God, Tom, Lou, thank you!

"Why wouldn't it come out easily?" I asked, confused.

"So, in 20% of Whipple surgeries, we find that the tumor has wrapped itself around the mesenteric artery, which goes to all of the intestine. If that's the case, we cannot continue with the operation."

This was the first time I heard about the mesenteric artery and silently thanked Cristina for never telling me this.

"Anyway, he is doing great and should be out of recovery in about two hours. Go for a walk! Get a bite to eat. He'll be in his room by 3 pm."

I was just about to get up when Will started asking questions I was praying he wouldn't. "So now he's all clear, right? Nothing else to worry about, right?" A huge lump formed in the pit of my stomach, knowing Cristina would not lie.

"Well, he has a much better chance at being ok now than if he hadn't had the Whipple," she answered.

"How much of a chance?" Will wanted to know. The knot in my tummy doubled in size.

"For the first year, there's a 27% survival rate, the second year it drops down to 17%, then to 5.4% at year five." Will struggled to breathe and all I wanted to do was hold him. Instead I said:

"That's right. And Frank is going to be one of the 5.4%, right Joanna?"

"Duh. Of course. You know your dad – nothing is going to take him down!" The absolute conviction in her voice made me look up, realizing that she was being completely truthful. She and I both knew that Frank would be ok. And now Will knew, too.

Joanna and I stayed at Frank's bedside while Will had to go back to New York with a heavy heart. He did not want to leave his Dad.

That evening, before I started banging away on my Tong Ren doll, I called LouLou to let her know the good news and to tell her about the mesenteric artery. The smile in her voice was unmistakable as she said:

"Yeah! I've been tapping on that thing for weeks now!!!"

# UPDATES

---

August 19th, 2008

----- *Original Message* -----
*From: juliette@centerofthought.com*
*To: Family and Friends*
*Sent: Tue Aug 19 08*
*Subject: First night update*

*Morning friends,*

*Frank had a very busy, but completely pain free night! He gets two ice cubes for breakfast, lunch and dinner and he isn't sharing any of them with me!!!! In just a little while, they'll put him on his feet. Amazing. Pls. know that he is not allowed to have any visitors for another 3 to 4 days. Love to all!*

August 20th, 2008

3 Days after the Whipple and Frank is feeling feisty!

*From: juliette@centerofthought.com*
*Sent: Wednesday, August 20, 2008 4:00 PM*
*To: Family and Friends*
*Subject: Update*

*Day 3 and all is going well! Frank's getting up 3 - 4 times a day for walks around the floor - very impressive. He can already have beverages and is feeling stronger already! Every day gets better and more comfortable. He's now sporting a 10" scar, 26 staples - very manly!!!! I've been with him pretty much 24/7 and last night, along with Joanna, we watched the movie: 'The Birdcage". Poor Frank, he was trying so hard not to laugh - all JoJo and I heard were snorts, hackles and giggles (yes, I think we heard a giggle!), followed by a very bad 4-letter word!*

*More tomorrow!*

*Love,*

*Juliette*

# PRAYING FOR A FART

---

August 22$^{nd}$, 2008

Frank was doing better than anyone who's ever had the Whipple (at least we were convinced of that). The second and third day, he was walking around the floor. On the 21$^{st}$, we went outside for a walk and on the 22$^{nd}$ he was walking up and down the stairs. Rob, Frank's godson, came to visit every day, which we always looked forward to. He brought with him a sense of calm and his easy going attitude was beautifully contagious. Dr. Ferrone came by every evening, making us her last visit. She along with belly would plop onto Frank's bed, telling us about her day and how absolutely fantastic Frank was doing and looking.

"Time to go home," Frank stated.

"Not yet. We need to know that everything is working in there" Cristina explained, pointing to Frank's stomach, which still had several tubes hanging out of it.

"How will we know?" I asked.

"As soon as he passes gas, he can go home." *Seriously?*

"Can I bring him some beans or sauerkraut to help the process?" I wanted to know.

After a few laughs, Cristina left and Frank and I tried to figure out a way to get him to fart.

Family and friends constantly emailed and texted us, trying to find out how Frank was doing. My reply was the same to all of them: "Pray for a fart, will explain later."

We woke up early Saturday and behold! We had a fart. I immediately ran outside to the nurses' station and asked one of them to inform Dr. Ferrone. The reply came back soon that we could pack our bags and go home, after the proper discharge procedure.

Donna, a nurse practitioner, came into our room to take out Frank's tubes. As she said hello, her eyes caught sight of the Tong Ren doll and she burst out: "You know Tom Tam?"

"Yes," I said. "Do you?"

"Yes! He saved my life 4 years ago. I had stage 4 breast cancer but am completely cured now." We hugged, happy to have met yet another of Tom's walking miracles, and went home along with our prescriptions for Prilosec, pain killers and digestive enzymes. Frank was back in our own bed and I was back in his arms. Everything was alright.

-------Original Message-------
*From: juliette@centerofthought.com*
*Date: 8/22/2008 10:40:24 AM*
*To: Family and Friends*
*Subject: Update*

*Morning!*

*The Doctors this morning said that NOBODY has EVER had a recovery like Frank! And, they do between 260 and 280 Whipples a year!!!! If his ass cooperates (literally.... 😀) he's coming home TOMORROW! It's unbelievable, isn't it?!*

*Love to all of you and pray for a fart or bowl movement (no joke, Rita)....*

*Isn't life something!!!!*

*Juliette*

Sunday, August 24<sup>th</sup>, 2008

It was an incredible morning. The sun was shining and the ocean glistened like a billion diamonds were scattered all over it. We grabbed the New York Times and the Boston Globe and sat in the welcoming warmth, enjoying our yard. Magie was thrilled to have us back home again, bestowing "dad" with big, wet kisses.

"THE NCI (NATIONAL CANCER INSTITUTE) AND THE ACS (AMERICAN CANCER SOCIETY) HAVE EMBARKED ON UNETHICAL TRIALS WITH 2 HORMONAL DRUGS, TAMOXIFEN AND EVISTA, IN ILL-CONCEIVED ATTEMPTS TO PREVENT BREAST CANCER IN HEALTHY WOMEN WHILE SUPPRESSING EVIDENCE THAT THESE DRUGS ARE KNOWN TO CAUSE LIVER AND OVARIAN CANCER RESPECTIVELY, AND IN SPITE OF SHORT TERM LETHAL COMPLICATIONS OF TAMOXIFEN AND IN SPITE OF TWO PUBLISHED LONG TERM STUDIES ON THE INEFFECTIVENESS OF TAMOXIFEN. THIS REPRESENTS MEDICAL MALPRACTICE VERGING ON THE CRIMINAL."

"IN SPITE OF THE BILLIONS OF DOLLARS SPENT ON THE WAR ON CANCER LAUNCHED BY PRESIDENT NIXON IN 1971, THERE HAS BEEN LITTLE IF ANY SIGNIFICANT IMPROVEMENT IN TREATMENT AND SURVIVAL RATES FOR MOST COMMON CANCERS, IN SPITE OF CONTRARY AND MISLEADING HYPE BY THE CANCER ESTABLISHMENT – THE NATIONAL CANCER INSTITUTE (NCI AND THE AMERICAN CANCER SOCIETY (ACS)."

"THE NATIONAL CANCER INSTITUTE AND THE AMERICAN CANCER SOCIETY HAVE MISLED AND CONFUSED THE PUBLIC AND CONGRESS WITH REPEATED FALSE CLAIMS THAT WE ARE WINNING THE WAR AGAINST CANCER – CLAIMS MADE TO CREATE PUBLIC AND CONGRESSIONAL SUPPORT FOR MASSIVE INCREASES IN BUDGETARY APPROPRIATIONS."

Samuel Epstein, M.D. from "The Politics of Cancer Revisited"

# MEET THE LYMPH NODE, YOUR GARBAGE COLLECTOR

Thursday, August 28th, 2008

We drove to Mass General to have Frank's staples removed. During the visit, we found out that the pathology results from the Whipple showed that three out of the nineteen lymph nodes that were tested came back positive with cancer. When I told Marie-Lou about this she said:

"That's great! The lymph nodes are the garbage collectors of the body and that's exactly where the cancer should be. Now, we just have to speed up the metabolism and get the lymph nodes cleaned out." I began tapping on the Triple Warmers 16 and 17 with a vengeance.

Over the weekend, Frank was riding the bike and lifting weights; nothing over five pounds though. The elliptical had to wait a few more days. Frank continued to heal beautifully and as far as work was concerned, they all thought he was out due to a minor stomach problem.

September 7th, 2008

*From: juliette@centerofthought.com*
*Sent: Sunday, September 07, 2008 4:16 PM*
*To: Family and Friends*
*Subject: Happy Sunday!*

*Hello everyone,*

*Well, the "good" times are over.... Frank's going back to work* 😊 *I was just getting used to having his now very little butt at home!*

*Not only does he feel good, but the 10" scar has basically disappeared! He's been exercising every morning and is anxious to pick up where he left off.*

*As important events happen, such as me not finishing my plate or our cat Moose spitting up a particularly impressive fur ball, I will continue to keep you posted and up to date!*

*Have a fantastic week!*

*Love to all,*

*Juliette*

# ANOTHER SCAN

Tuesday, September 16th, 2008

Today we went to Mass General Hospital in Chelsea for a CT scan to use as a benchmark for the chemo. Poor Frank had to gag down two bottles of Barium Sulfate disguised as a vanilla smoothie. The disgusting "disguise" left him gagging and sweating.

# GEMCITABINE (GEMZAR)

What follows is my personal belief validation in that chemotherapy is an experimental way to prolong death, not fight for life.

GEMCITABINE (GEMZAR): IN MAY, 1996, THE FDA APPROVED THE FIRST DRUG FOR THE TREATMENT OF PANCREATIC CANCER, GEMCITABINE (GEMZAR). FINAL APPROVAL WAS BASED ON TWO NON-RANDOMIZED PHASE II CLINICAL TRIALS. IN THE US TRIAL, THIS INVOLVED ONLY 44 PATIENTS. THERE WAS AN 11 PERCENT OVERALL RESPONSE RATE WITH A MEDIAN SURVIVAL TIME OF JUST 5.6 MONTHS [INVEST NEW DRUGS 1994;12:1229]. IN A EUROPEAN STUDY OF 34 PATIENTS, THERE WAS AN OVERALL RESPONSE RATE OF 6.3 PERCENT AND A MEDIAN SURVIVAL OF 6.3 MONTHS [BR J CANCER 1996;73:101-105].

THESE WERE SMALL, NON-RANDOMIZED TRIALS, AND SO IT IS IMPOSSIBLE TO SAY HOW THESE RESULTS COMPARE WITH NO TREATMENT. THE DRUG'S MANUFACTURER, ELI LILLY, REALIZED THAT IT COULD NOT CLAIM THAT GEMZAR WAS A LIFE-PROLONGING TREATMENT FOR PANCREATIC CANCER. BUT SINCE ONE-QUARTER OF PATIENTS TAKING GEMZAR EXPERIENCED AN IMPROVEMENT IN QUALITY OF LIFE, THE COMPANY REQUESTED, AND FDA GRANTED, PERMISSION TO MARKET THE DRUG BASED ON THIS BENEFIT.

FOR SEVERAL YEARS PRIOR TO APPROVAL, GEMZAR WAS MADE AVAILABLE TO PANCREATIC CANCER PATIENTS THROUGH A SPECIAL COMPASSIONATE USE AGREEMENT BETWEEN THE FDA AND THE COMPANY. LILLY SCIENTISTS LATER PUBLISHED AN ANALYSIS OF PATIENTS WHO RECEIVED GEMZAR IN THIS PROGRAM. OUT OF NEARLY 1,000 PATIENTS RECEIVING THE DRUG, 14 (ABOUT 1.4 PERCENT) WERE SAID TO HAVE HAD COMPLETE TUMOR RESPONSES. AN ADDITIONAL 10.6 PERCENT HAD PARTIAL RESPONSES. TAKEN TOGETHER, THESE ADD UP TO AN OVERALL RESPONSE RATE OF 12.0 PERCENT.

HOWEVER, THERE ARE PROBLEMS EVEN WITH THESE RESULTS, MODEST THOUGH THEY ARE. FIRST, THE ASSESSMENT OF RESPONSES WAS MADE BY "INDIVIDUAL INVESTIGATORS AND WERE NOT SUBJECTED TO INDEPENDENT REVIEW" [CANCER 1999;85:1261-1268]. THIS METHOD OF EVALUATION INTRODUCES POTENTIAL SOURCES OF ERROR AND BIAS INTO THE EVALUATION PROCESS. THE "INDIVIDUAL INVESTIGATORS" IN QUESTION INCLUDED DOCTORS WHO WERE NOT

NECESSARILY TRAINED IN RIGOROUSLY ASSESSING CLINICAL OUTCOMES. THEY WERE PRONE TO SUBJECTIVE IMPRESSIONS. A THOROUGH AND DISPASSIONATE EXAMINATION WOULD PROBABLY HAVE UNCOVERED MORE RESIDUAL OR METASTATIC DISEASE, THEREBY LOWERING THIS LOW RESPONSE RATE EVEN FURTHER.

FOR 2,380 PATIENTS ON WHOM SURVIVAL DATA WAS GATHERED, THE MEDIAN OVERALL SURVIVAL TIME AFTER STARTING GEMCITABINE WAS JUST 4.8 MONTHS, SLIGHTLY WORSE THAN IN THE CLINICAL TRIAL. ONLY 15 PERCENT SURVIVED TO ONE YEAR. THERE WAS NOTHING TO SUGGEST THAT THE RESPONSES CORRELATED WITH AN INCREASE IN OVERALL SURVIVAL.

ONE MUST ALSO QUESTION WHETHER THIS RELATIVELY EXPENSIVE NEW DRUG IS BETTER THAN THE LESS EXPENSIVE OLD DRUG THAT IT WAS MEANT TO REPLACE, FLUOROURACIL (5-FU). IN SOME UNCONTROLLED STUDIES, FLUOROURACIL ALONE PRODUCED RESPONSES UP TO 19 PERCENT WITH A MEDIAN SURVIVAL BETWEEN 4.2 TO 5.5 MONTHS – ALMOST IDENTICAL TO WHAT WAS ACHIEVED WITH GEMCITABINE [J CLIN ONCOL 1997;15:2403-2143].

GEMCITABINE RECEIVED ADDITIONAL APPROVAL IN AUGUST, 1998 FOR USE IN COMBINATION WITH THE OLDER DRUG, CISPLATIN, AS A FIRST-LINE TREATMENT OF PATIENTS WITH INOPERABLE, LOCALLY ADVANCED (STAGE IIIA OR IIIB) OR METASTATIC (STAGE IV) NON-SMALL CELL LUNG CANCER.

IN GREECE, THERE WAS A PHASE II STUDY IN 49 SUCH PATIENTS. THERE WAS 1 (2 PERCENT) COMPLETE AND 8 (16 PERCENT) PARTIAL RESPONSES. THE MEDIAN DURATION OF THE RESPONSE WAS 7 MONTHS AND THE MEDIAN SURVIVAL TIME WAS 11 MONTHS. HOW THESE RESULTS COMPARE TO NO FURTHER MEDICAL TREATMENT IS NOT KNOWN, SINCE THIS WAS NOT A RANDOMIZED OR PLACEBO-CONTROLLED TRIAL. THE OPTIMISTIC AUTHORS CALL THIS A "RELATIVELY ACTIVE SALVAGE REGIMEN" THAT "MERITS FURTHER INVESTIGATION" [ANN ONCOL 1998;9:1127-30\.

IN A SPANISH STUDY, THERE WERE 40 ASSESSABLE PATIENTS, AND 19 HAD A PARTIAL RESPONSE, FOR AN OVERALL RESPONSE RATE OF 47.5 PERCENT. THE MEDIAN SURVIVAL WAS 10.4 MONTHS [LUNG CANCER 1998;22:139-48].

GEMZAR IS ALSO BEING WIDELY USED TO TREAT STAGE IV BREAST CANCER. A PHASE II (NON-RANDOMIZED) STUDY AT THE CHARITE HOSPITAL IN BERLIN SHOWED THAT OUT OF 42 PATIENTS, THERE WERE NO COMPLETE RESPONSES. THERE WERE HOWEVER 6 PARTIAL RESPONSES AND 24 PATIENTS WITH STABLE DISEASE THAT LASTED 2 TO 9 MONTHS. THE OVERALL RESPONSE RATE WAS 14.3 PERCENT. THE MEDIAN SURVIVAL FOR ALL PATIENTS WAS 15.2 MONTHS. THERE WAS SEVERE TOXICITY IN FIVE PATIENTS WITH NAUSEA AND VOMITING, ONE PATIENT WITH DIARRHEA, ONE PATIENT WITH PAIN, ETC. THE

AUTHORS CALL THESE RESULTS "MODEST" [ANTICANCER DRUGS 1999;10:155-62].

IN ANOTHER 1996 BRITISH STUDY, OUT OF 40 EVALUABLE PATIENTS, THERE WERE 3 COMPLETE RESPONSES AND 7 PARTIAL RESPONSES, FOR AN OVERALL RESPONSE RATE OF 25.0 PERCENT. BUT THE MEDIAN SURVIVAL IN THIS STUDY WAS JUST 11.5 MONTHS [SEMIN ONCOL 1996;23S:77-81\. NOTICE THAT THE "RESPONSE RATE" WAS NEARLY DOUBLE THAT OF THE GERMAN STUDY, BUT MEDIAN SURVIVAL WAS FOUR MONTHS LESS. I ONCE AGAIN CALL THE READER'S ATTENTION TO THIS FAILURE OF RESPONSE RATES TO FAVORABLY CORRELATE WITH INCREASED SURVIVAL.

# ROUND ONE: FIRST CHEMO

Friday, September 19th, 2008

We met with Dr. Dave Ryan to go over the chemo schedule. Not a happy time for me. I had met so many people in the last few weeks that were explaining to me how devastatingly disastrous chemo can be. "Cancer doesn't kill people, Chemo does" is what I heard over and over again. But Dr. Ferrone was optimistic and so was Frank. I tried to talk Frank out of it a couple of times, but in the end understood that he wanted to do this and decided to support him in his decision to the best of my abilities.

They started out with Frank's blood work, then sent us up to the "chemo floor". Our chemo nurse, Theresa, was outstanding. She was as tall as me and had the same goofy sense of humor. What a blessing to be in the hands of someone not only capable, but also someone you like. Speaking of trust and like, Joanna became my weekly angel – chatting away with me and keeping it light while Frank was being poisoned. Not sure if I could have gone through eighteen treatments without her help. Her strong conviction that chemo was the best thing we could do was balancing my resolute hatred toward the thing.

# Juliette Guidara

Saturday, September 20<sup>th</sup>, 2008

*From: juliette@centerofthought.com*
*Sent: Saturday, September 20, 2008 8:00 AM*
*To: Family and Friends*
*Subject: Chemo No. 1 - DONE!*

*Good Morning Family & Friends,*

*Frank had his first chemo session yesterday, and except for taking up way too much time for "Mr. Not-Now-But-RIGHT-Now", it went really well.*

*We had a last minute oncologist-switch. Frank's surgeon, Dr. Ferrone whom we're all totally nuts about, somehow picked up that the chemistry wasn't there with his originally assigned oncologist and suggested that Frank meet with the director of the oncology wing on Thursday morning. The two of them hit it off immediately - Dr. Ryan was an English Major, Pre-Med Minor and spent just shy of 45 minutes with Frank teaching, explaining and educating. Very impressive. What's even more important to us is that Dr. Ryan has an open mind as far as Chemo is concerned and leans a bit more toward the European approach (start easy and see if more is needed as we go). In the US, each patient gets 1000 mg of chemo per m2 (square meter) - no matter what. He admitted that no Pharmaceutical company would sponsor studies where patients get less (for obvious monetary reasons) but he thinks that patients could easily take less w/out jeopardizing the effect. So instead of 1000 mg / m2, he started Frank with 750 mg/m2.*

*After we got home, Frank took a eucalyptus-infused steam bath (which he'll do every day to sweat out the poison) and then wolfed down 2 bowls of my very, very special spaghetti. Hey, since I became Italian last year, I learned that spaghetti is the cure for all aches, eh?*

*He didn't sleep all that well because he was too curious to see how his body would react (to the chemo, not the spaghetti) - it didn't. YEAH! Of course I'm tapping my arm off every day (Tong Ren) and oh - I forgot, the doctors NEVER saw a scar heal this well before!*

*17 more to go. Keep your thoughts and prayers going and I'll be back for more soon.*

*Love, Juliette & Frank*

# CHEMO REARS ITS UGLY HEAD

Monday, September 22$^{nd}$, 2008

Horrible day! I woke up to Frank calling my name at 5:00 a.m. His voice came from the bathroom so I immediately went in there. Frank was lying on the ice cold bathroom floor and could not move. I tried to get him up, away from the cold marble floor, but it was useless.

"It feels like every bone in my body is broken" he said. His right hand looked twice its size. I gave him a painkiller and put every warm blanket we own on and around him.

"How long have you been laying here, honey?" I asked, trying to keep my voice calm.

"For a couple of hours, I think. I didn't want to wake you up." Frank said.

After an hour of waiting for the pain to subside, he still couldn't move. At all. I had to keep going back to the bed and sit down, I was so nauseous with fear I was literally fighting passing out. We called Mass General and they immediately sent a prescription of heavy duty Oxycodone to our

Pharmacy. They said that the chemo might affect some of his old injuries. I practically flew to the pharmacy, calling them every two minutes to make sure they'd have it ready when I got there. After taking those, Frank started to feel better. I was worried sick that this reaction would be continuous and that he'd have to be on Oxycodone for the next five months. The next day, he felt better. The swelling had subsided and he could get around with little difficulties.

# ROUND ONE: SECOND CHEMO STEROIDS OR OXYCODONE?

---

Friday, September 26th, 2008

We found out that a small dose of steroids would eliminate the painful reaction. Steroids or Oxycodone? No brainer. Frank started taking the steroids in various doses the day of, and a couple of days post chemo. That night he lost sight in one eye for a little while (urgh – what now?!) and his breathing became irregular.

# GOING IN COLD, COMING OUT WARM

Saturday, September 27th, 2008

I drove a cold, sleepy and sluggish Frank to see Tom Tam in Haverhill. His acupuncture/ChiGong/Tong Ren/Tui Na appointment was at 2:30 pm. He came out of the room beaming, feeling warm and totally energized and ready to rumble. We called our friend Manny and went out to dinner with him and his girlfriend. Tom must have given him a bit too much energy, because instead of sleeping, Frank stayed up most of the night watching movies. Over the past months, the miracle stories we kept hearing at Tom's could no longer be ignored. People have opinions and are skeptical, which is great, but at the end of the day you cannot argue with blood nor results. After seeing many cancer patients who were sent home to die get better and better, we decided to become certified Tong Ren Practitioners! We took our first course on Sunday, the 28th and loved every minute of it. At one

175

point Frank started to get a little tired, and Tommie, during a break, fixed him right up!

During this entire time, we kept struggling with what to eat. First we went raw – which didn't sustain Frank. Now, I was making dry aged New York steaks every Friday night. Frank started to get low on iron so I thought this would be the best thing for him. While he was upstairs detoxing in the steam shower, I'd slave away in the kitchen. That was our weekly Friday night routine.

# GLORIA, ANGEL NUMBER THREE

I met Gloria while I was lying on a table, having volunteered to be the guinea pig for a cranial sacral massage demonstration. She was sitting right next to my head and as I looked up at her, I noticed her amazing eyebrows.

"You have the most perfect eyebrows I've ever seen," I blurted out.

"Julie Michaud", came the instant reply.

"We need to talk after this, do you have time?" I asked. She did and we bonded over eyebrow talk. Amazing how friendships form!

Angel number three called to see what was going on. I hadn't told her about Frank's condition because he really wanted to keep a tight lid on it, but she intuitively knew that something was going on and drilled a little bit. She was either a good driller, or I must have had another weak moment because I told her everything...

"Go online as soon as you can and check out the Hippocrates Health Institute in West Palm Beach, Florida. David (her husband) built the Oasis Spa there and he says it's incredible what they do for sick people."

Another door was shown to us. I went online, did my research, compared it to other health institutes around the country, and was convinced that Hippocrates' three week life change program was exactly what we needed. I told Frank all about it and we both agreed that after the last round of chemo, we'd go there to detox. Another plan in place, yippee!

# ROUND ONE: THIRD CHEMO

Friday, October 3rd, 2008


We felt much better about it having gained confidence in the steroids. Saw Tom on Saturday and again, went out to dinner, Frank feeling like a new man.


October 13th, 2008


-------- *Original Message* --------
*Subject: Gearing up for Round Two*
*From: juliette@centerofthought.com*
*Date: Mon, October 13, 2008 3:32 pm*
*To: Family and Friends*


*Hello all,*

*The first round of chemo resulted in 3:0 FRANK! Even though he had a couple of rough days during the first week of the first course (his body's immune system reacted very strongly to the poison, which was bad for Frank, but says a lot about his powerful immune system), he recovered quickly and as not-so-surprisingly-anticipated, is back to work full time now. I still throw a full blown temper tantrum once in a while, which is not pretty and rather loud in order to get his butt home early, but it's effects are sadly weakening on a daily basis. Kind of like the economy.*

*Now we're gearing up for round 2 which starts this Friday. So far, he's still on 75% of the recommended dosage which is terrific (less is more in this case!).*

*We spent the weekend farting around the yard, enjoying the warmth and the last bloom of our beloved flowers. Wouldn't you know that as soon as it came to "turd-patrol", Frank's energy shit the bed and he had to go lay down. Then it was up to Moose (cat) and me to scoop and toss, again. I would appreciate it if you guys could lay a little guilt trip on him next time you talk to him, perhaps speaking to the fact that anything to do with dog shit is a man's job after all!!!! I'll continue cleaning the litter box.*

*Thanks again for your continued prayers and well wishes - I keep getting asked to send out these updates but since everything is going so well, there's not much to say. So it's all y'all's fault for getting these silly little Christmas-Like-Chain-Letter-emails from me....*

*Love to all*

*Juliette*

# ROUND TWO: FIRST CHEMO

Friday, October 17<sup>th</sup>, 2008

Frank's blood work revealed a low iron count. I bought a bigger steak. To our huge joy, Will came up to spend the weekend with us. We dragged him along to meet Tom Tam and I think his exact words were: "You guys, are you shitting me?"

We spent a great weekend together and were sad to see him go on Sunday. We went to bed early that day because Frank had an important General Manager's meeting coming up. Nobody at his work (except for his assistant, the COO and the CFO) knew that he was undergoing chemo. They probably just thought he was slacking off, enjoying long weekends and a spectacular Fall.

# ROUND TWO: SECOND CHEMO BRING ON THE IRON!

---

Friday, October 24th, 2008

Frank's hemoglobin count was dipping lower as did his energy level. I tried to find every single iron rich food available and started shucking oysters and clams, bought mussels and started grilling slabs of red meat surrounded by tons of spinach, handing him dried apricots for dessert and making cream of buckwheat for breakfast.

# ROUND TWO: THIRD CHEMO

Friday, October 31st, 2008

Not to gross you out, but Frank's bowl movements had become very stinky again! Wasabi and Moose found this deliriously thrilling. Me, not so much. He brought it up to Dr. Ryan today and his enzyme intake was adjusted. Go, enzymes, go!

-------- *Original Message* --------
*Subject: Round Two: OVER!*
*From: juliette@centerofthought.com*
*Date: Tue, November 04, 2008 12:13 pm*
*To: Family and Friends*

*Hello everyone,*

*Ta daaaaaaaaaaaaaaaaaaaaaaaa. Round 2 is in the bag. Frank's feeling bet-*
*ter this week than ever and we're excited about the upcoming holiday season.*
*The third round consists of only two treatments (yippee) on Nov. 13th and*
*21st (I told the doc that I needed Frank's ass usable in order to participate in*
*the Thanksgiving Spirit (as in doing dishes and collecting doggie "gifts"). He*
*understood.*

*It's amazing how chemo works - Frank and I continue to be flabbergasted by*
*what's happening in his body. As you probably know, chemo affects mostly the*
*fast-changing-cells, such as Skin, Hair and the Blood Marrow. So after a treat-*
*ment, the skin on his thighs may burn for a few hours, or his hip might be sore,*
*etc. Nothing lasts long which allows us to watch what's going on with more of*
*a sense of curiosity, rather than fear. As long as his body reacts, it means his*
*immune system is kicking chemo ass! We like that. As far as his hair - it's never*
*looked better. I'm thinking of signing up for a couple of rounds.....*

*Love to all and God bless! Juliette*

# LIFE AFTER DEATH

---

Monday, November 10, 2008

Frank was in Las Vegas for a Restaurant Conference and I had some time to reflect. Marie-Lou and I spent several hours together talking about life, death, and life after death. I always knew that losing the physical body did not mean the end:

On December 19th, 1993, my Grandmother who was also my Godmother, passed away. Luise was as close to a saint as anyone could be. Every morning at 4:30, she went to the nunnery for Mass. At 10:30, she went to attend Mass in church. At 4:00 pm, she went back to the church to say her prayers. She and God were like, you know, "like this". She had come to me in my dreams a couple of weeks earlier to say goodbye. It was such a real experience that I woke up sobbing. She was not sick though and the more I woke up, the more I convinced myself that it was, well, just a dream.

That night, I was sitting on the couch in our penthouse apartment in Beverly Hills, watching TV. We had a bar just to the left and up a couple of stairs on a landing. It was a small room, maybe 15 feet wide. On the right were glass shelves featuring champagne flutes, red and white wine glasses, cognac snifters and shot glasses. Directly across the room was a big mirror. All of a sudden, I saw two champagne flutes, the center ones in a row of 18, fly across the room and shatter against the mirror. My first thought was Earthquake, but it wasn't, none of the other glasses moved, not even a tiny bit. There was a force behind throwing those flutes across the room that was rather strange, to say the least. I cleaned up the mess and returned to my movie, wondering what that was all about.

The next morning, I got a call from my mom.

"JouJou, I am so sorry to have to tell you that grandma died yesterday." She said.

"When, mom?"

"Right after lunch." She answered.

"What time?"

"It was right around 12:30 pm, why?" She asked, curious. *12:30 pm Swiss time was 3:30 am LA time. That's just a couple of hours after the flutes flew!*

"How did it happen, Mom?" I asked.

"Well, it was kind of strange. A couple of days ago, she called all of us kids, saying that she wanted to invite us over for lunch. Everybody was busy and since we don't exactly live close by, we tried to get out of it, but mamma insisted. So we all went, me, Peter, Paul, Agatha, Jules and Ernst. It was a terrific lunch, which she lovingly cooked and served to all of us. After we were done eating, we went into the living room when mamma told us that she was going to take a nap on the sofa back in the dining room. We all sat talking and catching up, when all of a sudden the chandelier

188

started going around in circles, slowly at first, then rapidly gaining speed. Peter, Jules and Paul climbed halfway onto the piano and its chair, trying to stop the thing but they couldn't! The three of them could not stop it from spinning around and around. (You have to know that Peter, Jules and Paul are big ol' Swiss Mountain Men!) Agatha and I went into the dining room, where we found mamma in blissful sleep, gone."

"Mom?" I asked.

"Yes honey?"

"Grandma has a really strange sense of humor. Last night, just a few hours after her passing, she threw two very expensive champagne flutes across the wall here in Beverly Hills!"

"She did not! Really?" Mom laughed.

"She sure did. You and dad are not going to pull the same crap, are you?!" I asked, laughing and crying at the same time.

"We'll go after the cheap stuff, JouJou, don't worry." She replied.

My Grandma must have somehow convinced God to let her give us a sign that she was still around, somewhere.

189

# ROUND THREE: FIRST CHEMO NUTS AND SEAWEED

Thursday, November 13th, 2008

Frank was low in energy and electrolytes. His enzymes were still being adjusted and I found out that fresh coconut water contains a ton of enzymes as well as electrolytes. Thankfully, we have a Whole Foods Market not far away where fresh baby coconuts are always available. Opening the damn things, however, is an art in itself. It took me forever to figure it out – first, I'd go outside with a hammer and a screwdriver, hacking away – running all over the yard chasing the damn nut. Paul, Marie-Lou's husband, came to my rescue. After having nearly hammered my fingers to mush, he sent me a video on YouTube that showed how to gently and easily open the coconuts. Off I was to get a meat cleaver and voila! Bang, bang bang, open Sesame, open!

I also remembered from my yearly stays at La Costa in Carlsbad that seaweed is highly detoxifying. I went online and ordered organic seaweed baths from Benedetta. Every Friday afternoon, when we got home from chemo, I ran a bath. Now –baths are relaxing and enjoyable, right? Wrong. This seaweed bath looked and smelled like a toxic waste dump! It was absolutely disgusting; but highly effective. Frank's nose was even more sensitive to smells due to the chemo and the first time I asked him to step into the "sewer water", he flat out refused. So I jumped in first and added some eucalyptus drops, convincing him of the tremendous health benefits. Holding his nose, he gingerly stepped in.

"Oh my God, this really stinks, Juliette!" he yelled over the jets.

"I know, I have a nose, too! But it's going to pull a lot of the toxins out of you, so hang in there for 20 minutes, ok?"

It was freezing out, but the only way Frank could cope with the stench was to stick his head out the window. Amidst all the drama surrounding the chemo, we still found ways to laugh our seaweed covered butts off.

"Only twelve more baths to go, honey" I couldn't help it. If looks could kill…

# ROUND THREE: SECOND CHEMO

Friday, November 21st, 2008

Today we told Dr. Ryan about our plans to go to the Hippocrates Health Institute and asked if he could write a prescription for it. "Unfortunately, I can't" was his reply. He wasn't very optimistic about us going, stating his concerns and doubts about anything drastically alternative. But, our mind was made up, prescription or not.

Frank's body started to adjust to the chemo and the side effects were diminishing. He was still very cold – nothing a nice, relaxing seaweed bath couldn't take care of...

Saturday, November 22nd, 2008

Frank took a long steam shower after which we headed off to see Tom. It's truly amazing to see the change in Frank. Tired, weak and cold going in, strong, warm and full of energy coming out! Very cool!

# HAPPY THANKSGIVING

Thursday, November 27th, 2008

Happy Thanksgiving! We went over to Joanna's house and had a nice time surrounded by family. I appeared positive and happy, while deep inside I was a hurting puppy. Holidays have a way of making everything much worse, don't they? For me, they are a memory benchmark and I couldn't help but wonder if Frank would ever see another Thanksgiving.

By that time however, I had learned to not let my mind control me as much. Marie-Lou and I had been talking a lot about the mind lately, and how it has a tendency to "drive" us, if we let it. LouLou shared her work with me, which she calls "Mindshifting." Over the past few years, I have incorporated it into my hypnotherapy practice and have seen mind blowing results.

# MINDSHIFTING

Based on Marie-Lou Kuehne-Millerick's Work
http://www.synergy-healing.com

UNTIL WE LEARN TO SEE THE MIND AND INTELLECT FOR WHAT IT IS, WE ARE DRIVEN BY THOUGHTS, OWNED BY CONCEPTS, ASSUMPTIONS AND CONCLUSIONS AND SPIN WITH THE EMOTIONS THAT ARE THE CONSEQUENCE OF THIS MECHANISM.

We cannot simply stop the mind from doing "it's thing", that's why we dream at night. Thoughts come whether we want them to or not.

What typically happens is a continuum from thought to action. As in: Action – Reaction. For example, you might wake up in the morning, the thought of a donut appears in your head, and before you know it, you've got your car keys in your hand and you're running out the door to Dunkin Donuts.

What I teach my clients is Action – Pause – Choice – Reaction. Meaning: The thought of a donut shows up. Now pause and look at it for what it is and determine whether it is a thought worthy of engaging with. What is your goal? What do you want? If you are lean and thin and want a sugar rush – then go ahead, engage with the thought and have at it. However, if your goal is to lose a few pounds and become radiantly healthy, dismiss the thought! It's as simple as imagining that you have a virtual remote control in your hand. A thought comes, you push the pause button. Look at it and evaluate its purpose. Then make a decision based on whether this thought serves your purpose. If it does not, change the channel and watch a different scene unfold, one starring you doing something that is healthy and good for you. Create the thought of an apple instead! Thoughts are like birds flying around, looking for a place to nest. I chose to invite nightingales, hummingbirds, parakeets, macaws and butterflies to come into my mind, my "aviary". The vultures can find another place to nest!

In my case, I have trained my mind to disengage with fearful thoughts. All those "what if's…" serve absolutely no purpose in my life. I also know that nothing is ever as it appears; so why worry about assumptions? When I get scared, I immediately dump the fear at God's feet, he knows what to do with it. I have also learned that wherever there is faith, there is no room for fear. However, in the absence of faith, there is fear. Besides, it says: "Thy Will Be Done", not mine.

IN 1986, MCGILL CANCER CENTER SCIENTISTS SENT A QUESTIONNAIRE TO 118 DOCTORS WHO TREATED NON-SMALL-CELL LUNG CANCER. MORE THAN ¾ OF THEM RECRUITED PATIENTS AND CARRIED OUT TRIALS OF TOXIC DRUGS FOR LUNG CANCER. THEY WERE ASKED TO IMAGINE THAT THEY THEMSELVES HAD CANCER, AND WERE ASKED WHICH OF SIX CURRENT TRIALS THEY THEMSELVES WOULD CHOOSE. SIXTY-FOUR OF THE SEVENTY NINE RESPONDENTS WOULD NOT CONSENT TO BE IN A TRIAL CONTAINING CISPLATIN, A COMMON CHEMOTHERAPY DRUG. FIFTY EIGHT FOUND ALL THE TRIALS UNACCEPTABLE.

THEIR REASON:

"THE INEFFECTIVENESS OF CHEMOTHERAPY AND ITS UNACCEPTABLE DEGREE OF TOXICITY."

From the Article: Chemotherapy: Snake-Oil Remedy?

# CA19-9 >1!

Frank didn't have to go in for chemo this week. I couldn't remember why but was thrilled! One less toxic infusion; yippee!

-------- *Original Message* --------
*Subject: Entering the Second Half*
*From: juliette@centerofthought.com*
*Date: Fri, December 05, 2008 9:41 am*
*To: Family and Friends*

*Hello all,*

*Today is the first treatment of the second half. Only 9 more to go.*

*Frank is doing exceptionally well (except for a stupid cold). And here is the GREAT NEWS..... Ready? You might want to sit down. Oh, you are sitting down. Right.*

*Frank's cancer marker (the measured protein output by cancerous cells measured in the blood) which is typically between 30 and 400 in pancreatic cancer patients, is less than 1! Yup, >1!!!!!!!!!!!!!!!*

*Happy, Happy Holidays!*

SS: "EVERYONE POINTS TO LANCE ARMSTRONG AND HIS REMARKABLE SUCCESS WITH TESTICULAR CANCER AND CHEMOTHERAPY. HE IS LITERALLY THE POSTER BOY FOR THE SUCCESS OF CHEMO. THE WAY I FOUND OUT ABOUT YOU WAS READING AN ARTICLE YOU WROTE THAT CHEMO REALLY ONLY WORKS FOR THREE KINDS OF CANCER: CHILDHOOD LEUKEMIA, SOME LYMPHOMAS, AND TESTICULAR CANCER."

NG: "THE WAY LANCE ARMSTRONG HAS BEEN PROMOTED BY THE CHEMO INDUSTRY IS REALLY UNFORTUNATE, AND I'M REALLY SADDENED THAT A MAN OF THAT CHARACTER WOULD ALLOW HIMSELF TO BE PROMOTED THAT WAY. TESTICULAR CANCER IS A RARE CANCER, NOT THAT MANY CASES EACH YEAR. THERE ARE 210,000 CASES OF BREAST CANCER DIAGNOSED YEARLY, AND ONLY 10,000 TO 15,000 CASES OF TESTICULAR. IT'S JUST NOT THAT COMMON, AND YOU ARE CORRECT THAT IT IS ONE OF THE FEW CANCERS THAT RESPONDS TO CHEMO. HODGKIN'S IS THE OTHER ASIDE FROM THE THREE YOU MENTIONED. THE FACT OF THE MATTER IS THAT FOR ALL THE MAJOR CANCER KILLERS – METASTATIC BREAST, LUNG, PROSTATE, AND PANCREATIC – CHEMOTHERAPY DOES ABSOLUTELY NOTHING...ZERO. THERE IS NO EVIDENCE THAT THOSE CHEMO DRUGS IN METASTATIC DISEASE PROLONG SURVIVAL SIGNIFICANTLY. IF THEY DO, IT'S A COUPLE OF MONTHS. SO TO GENERALIZE HIS EXPERIENCE TO CHEMOTHERAPY SUCCESS IN GENERAL IS A DISSERVICE. IT'S NOT SCIENTIFICALLY ACCURATE NOR HONEST. IT TRULY GIVES FALSE HOPE."

Interview with Dr. Nicholas Gonzales
from "Knockout" by Suzanne Somers

# ROUND FOUR: FIRST CHEMO

Friday, December 5th, 2008

While Joanna and I were sitting next to Frank in the "chemo room", a very friendly volunteer knocked on our door. She had a jewelry-making-kit with her and asked us if we were up to making some fun jewelry. How nice! We immediately began beading bracelets and were beautifully distracted. Mass General kept pleasantly surprising us.

The remaining chemo infusions were pretty uneventful. Frank was getting used to always being cold and he continued to lose weight, which was puzzling to us since his appetite was as ferocious as ever.

# MERRY CHRISTMAS

Thursday, December 25th, 2008

Christmas was a perfect way for Frank to relax and take it easy. He'd been working non-stop (except for the Friday afternoon chemo dates) and still, no one at his office knew what he was going through, except for his Assistant Diane Moynihan, his COO Roger Zingle, his CFO Louis Psallidas and Ed Soulier in H.R. who had to deal with all the health insurance claims.

I cooked my guts out and had everyone over at the house. Again, there were a few moments of worries – *what if this is Frank's last Christmas? How would I ever be able to celebrate Christmas again?* Then my faith and mind shifting techniques kicked in and I was able to celebrate with a grateful heart and a positive mind. It slowly dawned on me that whenever my faith was low, the fear grew. Again, in the absence of faith is fear!

# HAPPY NEW YEAR

---

December 31st, 2008

We were sitting at the bar of the Top of the Hub, sipping bubbly. This is one of our favorite restaurants in Boston. Raphael, the General Manager and our friend, arranged for a corner table and together with Manny and his girlfriend we said "Good Riddance" to 2008 and "Hey Howdy" to 2009. We were all in agreement that this was going to be a fantastic year.

# GETTING READY FOR HIPPOCRATES

I was getting more and more excited about our trip to the Hippocrates Health Institute. We tried again to get support from Mass General, this time turning to Cristina:

*From: juliette@centerofthought.com*
*Sent: Wednesday, February 04, 2009 1:58 PM*
*Subject: From Frank and Juliette Guidara, for Doc. Ferrone*

*Howdy Doc,*

*How is your little boy? Frank and I were amazed at how fabulous you looked when we ran into you. We're so happy for you and your family.*

*As you know, Frank and I are booked at the Hippocrates Health Institute in West Palm Beach for 3 weeks, March 15 - April 4th.*

*As you can imagine, Frank has not come up for air, working 12-hour days. On Feb. 13th is his last chemo infusion (yippee!). There are many reasons we are going, mainly to rest, boost his immune system through healthy exercise and nutritional support, oxygen treatments and various other complementary medical support modalities.*

*It's going to be tough for Frank to tell his executive team that he's taking 3 weeks off... he's never done that in his life. So we were wondering if you'd consider writing him a prescription. This is not just a spa... it's run by 2 doctors and an oncologist. But again, the main reason is the man needs some R&R! Here's their website - check it out when you have a minute: www.hippocratesinst.org.*

*Lets us know what you think!*

Cristina responded immediately and we got our prescription.

# LAST CHEMO

---

-------- *Original Message* --------
*Subject: One More!!!!!!!!!!!!!*
*From: juliette@centerofthought.com*
*Date: Wed, February 11, 2009 8:42 am*
*To: Family and Friends,*

*This is it.... Friday is Frank's last chemo infusion (big-ass-yeepeeeee hurray and hallelujah!!!!!). His blood work is off the charts and he's feeling great. The only thing that was a challenge was a wee bit of anemia; nothing the MOI couldn't handle... I immediately called my Mom to get her chicken liver recipe and behold, Frank who vowed to never eat another liver of any kind, gobbled down a whole plate. Granted, my Mom's recipe is comprised of 1/2 gallon of cream, 1/2 gallon of cognac and 1 liver hidden in a mound of buttered mashed potatoes, but still..... Then my Dad sent me a lentil recipe that's to live for.... combine that w/ cantaloupe juice, wheat grass shots, spinach and plant-extract iron, and a beautiful thing happened. Blatte, what do you think? Ready to move in w/ us?....*

*We plan on celebrating like stupid on Saturday and look forward to a blessed, happy and healthy future.*

*Know that we couldn't have made it through this without your prayers, love and support. To all of you, we thank you from the bottom of our hearts.*

*Love Always,*

*Juliette & Frank*

# ARMED BUT NO BATTLE

Monday, March 2nd, 2009

We met, once again, with Dr. Dave Ryan. I knew what to expect and I was ready for battle. The standard follow-up protocol prescribes CT scans every 3 months, which I was absolutely not happy about. Each CT scan of the abdomen has the equivalence of 3.3 years of natural radiation exposure. Besides, the anxiety before and after the scans was not something we wanted to subject ourselves to. We weren't about to give this cancer all this attention and energy. I was ready to fight and argue, which goes against everything I am. But this was too important and I was not going to back down!

Dr. Ryan entered our room and as I was about to leap at his throat, he smilingly said:

"Well, I don't think you're going to want to do the CT scans every 3 months, which is fine. But I'd like you to come in for a blood test every 6 months, would that be ok?"

215

I stood there like an empty wet sock, absolutely speechless. Frank found my expression highly amusing.

"Sounds great, Doc," he said, and then thanked him for being intuitively accommodating and admirably open minded.

# A CLEAN BILL
# OF HEALTH

---

*From: juliette@centerofthought.com*
*Sent: Tuesday, March 03, 2009 5:10 PM*
*To: Family and Friends*
*Subject: One More Update*

*It is with tears of joy streaming down my face that I'm sending you this email.*

*Frank had the mandatory cat scan last Friday to determine the status of his pancreas, liver and lungs, as well as any potential damage from chemo. We met with the oncologist and the surgeon yesterday and were given an absolute clean bill of health!!!!!!! The scan and his blood are perfect. My warrior-hubby, along with God and all his angels here on earth, did it; he fought and he won.*

*Now if you're thinking that we're going on vacation to celebrate, you're right. If you're thinking the Ritz or a fabulous hotel on the beach in an exotic part of the world, you're soooooooo wrong :) Instead of slurping Bahama Mamas, savoring succulent steaks and munching on chocolate covered strawberries, we're gonna gag down gallons of green juice, liter after delicious (yuck) liter of*

217

*wheat-grass and bundles of organic raw living foods at the Hippocrates Health Institute in FL. The purpose is to completely detox from the chemo and to bring his immune system back to full force.*

*This has been one hell of a year. Once again, we thank you all for your support, encouragement, love and loyalty. Now go out and have one on us!!!!!*

*Love always,*

*Juliette & Frank*

**CONTRIBUTION OF CHEMO TO 5-YEAR SURVIVAL IN AUSTRALIA: 2.3%, IN US 2.1%. NO CONTRIBUTION TO 5-YEAR SURVIVAL: 97.7%**

**Graeme Morgan, MD and Robyn Ward, MD from the Australia Study**

Thursday, March 12th, 2009

I couldn't wait to get out of town! The weather was still miserable and the Florida sunshine yelled and screamed my name. We flew to Miami where Gloria and David picked us up. We spent two wonderful days with our friends, enjoying great food, fantastic wine and lots of healing laughs.

# HIPPOCRATES
# HEALTH INSITUTE

Sunday, March 15<sup>th</sup>, 2009 – Saturday, April 4<sup>th</sup>, 2009

March 15<sup>th</sup>, 2009 – Arriving at Hippocrates Health Institute, W. Palm Beach, FL

We went for a "last real meal" which consisted of nachos, beer and Reuben's before Gloria and David dropped us off at Hippocrates. It's a beautifully landscaped, peaceful place in West Palm Beach. There were quotes from the bible in the "living room" and I felt instantly at ease. We arrived just in time for the 4:00 pm green juice which, as a beer chaser, we found downright disgusting!

The Hippocrates Health Institute was originally founded by the "Godmother of Wheatgrass", Ann Wigmore. Ann first cured herself of her many illnesses, then started to treat sick animals and eventually people. Wheatgrass is the most important aspect of the Hippocrates Health Institute. Here are some excerpts from "The Wheatgrass Book" by Ann Wigmore: Wheatgrass...

*"increases red blood cell count, lowers blood pressure... It cleanses the blood, organs and gastrointestinal tract of debris. It stimulates metabolism and bodily enzyme systems in enriching the blood by increasing red blood cell count, and in dilating the blood pathways throughout the body, reducing blood pressure."*

*"stimulates the thyroid, correcting obesity, indigestion, etc... The thyroid gland is also stimulated and normalized by the use of wheatgrass juice – an important step toward the correction of obesity, indigestion and a host of other complaints."*

*"restores alkalinity to the blood... Wheatgrass has an alkalizing effect on the blood. Its abundance of alkaline minerals helps reduce over acidity in the blood. It can be used to relieve many internal pains. It has been used successfully to treat peptic ulcers, ulcerative colitis, constipation, diarrhea, and other complaints of the gastrointestinal tract."*

*"powerful detoxifier and liver and blood protector...* The enzymes and amino acids found in wheatgrass can protect us from carcinogens like no other food or medicine can. It strengthens our cells, detoxifies the liver, bloodstream and chemically neutralizes environmental pollutants."

*"fights tumors and neutralizes toxins...* Recent studies show that wheatgrass juice has a powerful ability to fight tumors without the usual toxicity of drugs that also inhibit cell-destroying agents. The many active compounds found in grass juice can cleanse the blood and neutralize and digest toxins in our cells."

*"whether you have a cut finger you want to heal or you desire to lose five pounds...* Enzymes must do the actual work. The life and abilities of the enzymes found naturally in our bodies can be extended if we help them from the outside by adding exogenous enzymes, like the ones found in wheatgrass juice."

Today, the Hippocrates Health Institute is run by Dr. Brian R. Clement, who earned his BS in Biochemistry at the University of Miami, became a certified nutritionist and received a Ph.D. in nutrition from St. Marina University. He then obtained his NMD from The University of Science, Art and Technology. He has been the director of Hippocrates Health Institute since 1980.

Brian is a very dynamic, highly passionate teacher. If you ever get the chance to hear him speak, take it. He travels worldwide, generously sharing his knowledge and approach towards a healthy lifestyle.

Our first day involved getting our blood work done, as a comparison basis for the same test done again three weeks into the program. As they say, blood doesn't lie. Our initial life blood analysis with Annemarie, Brian's beautiful wife, was totally fascinating because we got to watch our live blood on a big screen. We saw our red blood cells which were somewhat clumped together, a few beautiful white blood cells strolling about and some other "good guys" marching around. *But then, oh gag me, what was that?!*

"Annemarie, what is THIS?" I yelled, pointing my finger at the screen, horrified by the disgusting, furry looking "wart-thingy-with-teeth" running around my blood.

"That," Annemarie said, smiling, "is a parasite."

"Get it out of me," I pleaded.

Frank too had parasites, as we pretty much all do. But knowing they exist and coming nose to snout with one is a whole different experience, at least it was for me. I couldn't wait to start the Paragon program and almost swallowed my first two pills along with the cotton padding.

Over the next three weeks, we learned more about nutrition and the human body than we could have ever dreamed of. We started every morning with a shot of wheatgrass, followed by some kind of exercise; walk or run, Pilates, Rebound, Stretch & Strengthen, TaiChi/ChiGong, Pool Exercises, weights or stationary equipment. Classes started generally at 9:00 a.m. and went all day. Frank underwent daily oxygen and infrared treatments as well as vitamin implants, while we both enjoyed H-Wave, Cranial Sacral and neuromuscular treatments.

Breakfast consisted of fresh green juice for me, "buckwheaties" (dehydrated buckwheat in buckwheat milk) or almond milk for Frank. He got to eat a little more because he was already down to 168 pounds and weight loss is a major concern for pancreatic cancer patients.

The lunch buffet was open from 12:30 pm to 1:30 pm and consisted of every imaginable sprout there is. In addition, there were always some other yummy raw food treats available, all organic and with no sugar. Initially, Frank and I pigged out on the raw olives because they were the only salty food around and had the most taste. A close second were radishes drenched in Bragg's liquid amino acids (a great salt substitute) and crunchy little peppers.

The dinner buffet was open from 5:30 pm to 6:30 pm and consisted of more sprouts, and lettuces, and other raw delicacies. In addition, fresh green juices were served three times a day and after getting used to them, we started to look forward to their arrival every few hours. The basic green juice consists of organic cucumber, celery, sunflower and sweet pea sprouts.

Twice daily, we also got to do implants. Don't know about those? Let me tell you. You press about four ounces of fresh wheatgrass into a cup, which you bring back to your room. Then you squat over a "diaper mat" and give yourself a warm water enema. After you pretty much crap your brains out, you implant the wheatgrass juice, enema style, and hold it for as long as you can. If you make it through 10 minutes without blowing up, the wheatgrass gets absorbed into your blood stream and that's a beautiful thing! As a side note – if you ever decide to take the three week life change program at Hippocrates, either get your own room or make damn sure that you are very, very, very close with whomever you go with!

A particularly interesting evening was when Victoras Kulvinskas spoke. The guy is a true genius and I highly recommend his books. Frank and I both had the privilege of meeting with him individually the next day. What a revelation that was!

# HELLO WEIRD
# HEALING CRISIS!

The day after my detox crisis from hell.  Much better now.

One day, about a week and a half into the program, my detox-healing-crisis was in full force. It started out with me laying in bed, sobbing and feeling absolutely miserable. I had had it with eating grass and I flat out refused to eat. I slumped off to a secluded spot and got downright suicidal – not that I was going to kill myself, but I actually begged God to bring me home. I felt that Frank knew what he had to do now to get better and that my job, as his life saving angel, was over. Frank found me a few hours later, obviously concerned. I told him what was going on inside of me and how I was feeling; he got more concerned. We talked for a while, him reassuring me while I was getting more and more depressed and weird, until it was time for another damn implant. I slouched off, miserable, and asked him not to come into the room for at least half an hour. I needed some privacy and was sick and tired of having to squat and crap within eyesight and hearing distance of my husband.

I was just ready to literally blow my guts out when Frank walked in the door.

"!$#%!" I screamed. I just couldn't help it. I had had it. Frank mumbled something and immediately retreated back to the safety of wherever he came from.

I tried to take a nap but couldn't sleep. All of a sudden, I started to feel better. From one minute to the next, I was back to being my happy, positive self. I'd never experienced such a drastic change in my behavior but decided it wasn't worth examining. The crisis was over and I was hungry and looking forward to my grass buffet. When a somewhat reluctant Frank found me at one of the many dinner tables, I was surrounded by our recently made friends and was in my glory, telling joke after joke, cracking them all up, smiling from ear to ear. I'm sure that must have been one of those *"women!"* moments for him.

That night, just like every other night, we sat in the warm mineral bath for what seemed like hours (which you are not supposed to do). But the warm water felt so good and so healing that I could barely get myself to get out. If Frank hadn't insisted, I would have spent every night in there, blissfully floating around. During these relaxing baths, we met and bonded with great people. There was Les who'd lost his wife due to a hospital screw up and Sharon and Charles Pfahl – he is an amazing artist and she a total sweetheart. To this day we are in close contact with them.

I took some notes while at Hippocrates that I would like to share with you. You will find them on Pages 291-304. I know that you will find them very interesting.

Towards the end of the second week, Frank lost eight pounds and I was down about twelve. The food started to get really mundane but since we were never hungry, who cared? The funny thing is that when you feed your body what it really needs, wants and craves, the hunger goes away. When you eat junk, you are never fully satisfied because your body keeps trying to communicate with you that it needs real nutrition. It is true that we are an overfed, but under-nourished nation.

# CECILIA, ANGEL NUMBER FOUR

One particular morning, everyone seemed to be in a bad mood, even Dr. Michael Hamilton who taught our ChiGong and meditation class every morning. Frank and I made it a point, every morning, to go to his class. There's something very special about the man and he is a brilliant teacher. That morning however, he made some snotty remark and at the end of the class he apologized for being an arrogant jerk.

As we walked out, I couldn't help but say, with a gentle smile:

"Doc, you're not an arrogant jerk, but you can be a pompous ass."

The next morning, Michael invited us to his home for dinner! Go figure. He said that his wife Cecilia was a raw food expert and that he'd like for us to meet her. He picked us up and heaven's gate opened to our long deprived taste buds.

Here was Angel Number Four. Cecilia is probably the most energetic, sweet, helpful person I've ever met. She immediately began spoiling us with delicious hibiscus tea served in red wine glasses, followed by an incredible dinner consisting of a crunchy salad, followed by dehydrated coconut crepes stuffed with veggies and shiitake mushrooms, and some kind of cheesecake and ice cream for dessert. Now – none of these foods were cooked, they were all raw and vegan. A whole new world opened up to me and I started to get excited.

*We can live on this!* I thought. The grass diet, I knew, would not last for very long, but this food was an entirely different story. As the evening progressed, we bonded and an amazing friendship was born. Cecilia Hubene, in addition to being a raw food chef and an international attorney, is also a very talented artist. Her paintings have been exhibited all around the world and all I can say is that without any training whatsoever, her gift can only come from the Divine. If you're into divine art, check out her website at: www.cecilehubene.com. For her advice on health, wellness and nutrition, go to www.foods2heal.com.

A couple of days later, me armed with a buzillion questions, we were invited back for a second dinner. Again, it was a beautiful evening, Michael giving a private ChiGong class to Frank in the living room, while I picked poor Cecilia's brain to bits and pieces in the kitchen. Cecilia even gave me some tasty raw salad dressing to take back to HHI, which I happily shared with our newly made friends.

# GOING HOME

Leaving Hippocrates, detoxed and looking fabulous!

Soon, we'd have to go home. The anxiety about keeping us raw, vegan and fed started to build. I knew that I would be solely responsible for keeping this raw food diet going due to Frank's time restraints. I had heard about a guy in Boston who grows organic sprouts. I called Randy Jacobs, a terrific guy and asked him if he could help us.

"Of course I can!" was the immediate, helpful reply. "Based on what you have told me, I will bring you 7 bags of wheatgrass, 7 bags of sunflower sprouts and 3 bags of sweet pea sprouts every Sunday evening, ok?"

"Ok," green juice done! Finding organic cucumbers and celery was not going to be a problem.

That afternoon Frank and I realized that we would need another suitcase to accommodate all of our new vitamins and supplements. Gloria and David immediately volunteered to take us to Target. I guess we weren't exactly a joy to be around, because suddenly, we heard Gloria hootin' and hollering from an isle far away. We went to see what the commotion was all about and there they were, Gloria and David, engaged in the most ridiculous hula hoop dance. We grabbed our own hula hoops and joined the insanity, laughing our butts off.

By the time we left Hippocrates, I weighed 148 pounds and Frank was down to 160 pounds. We felt confidently educated and extremely committed to this new way of living!

# A LITANY OF
# SUPPLEMENTS

---

April 2009

We got home and unpacked, immediately organizing our vitamins. Frank's daily regiment was as follows:

Morning Vitamins:

1 HHI (Hippocrates Health Institute) Life Give Men's Formula Multi Vitamin
1 HHI Life Give Ocean Energy
10 HHI Life Give Chlorella
5 HHI Life Give Power Powder
1 HHI Life Give B12-Forte
1 HHI Life Give D3
4 HHI Life Give Biotic Guard
1 Super ToCoQ10 (200 mg)
1 Nordic Nat'l. Complete Omega 3,6,9

Evening Vitamins:

1 HHI Life Give Men's Formula (Multi Vitamin)
1 HHI Life Give Ocean Energy
10 HHI Life Give Chlorella
5 HHI Life Give Power Powder
1 HHI Life Give D3

And with a meal, he took 1 Turmeric Force 400 mg and digestive enzymes.

# GOING RAW, AGAIN!

I told Marie-Lou and Paul about our commitment to be 100% raw. They immediately showed up with a Green Power Juicer, a dehydrator and Alissa Cohen's Raw Cook Book.

Lou and I, for the second time, went through every cabinet in our kitchen and tossed out bag after bag of food. Everything that was canned, packaged, bagged, frozen or contained sugar or salt was either given away or thrown out. You've never seen a kitchen or a fridge this empty… Then we went to Whole Foods and stocked up on Braggs, Nama Shoyu, Almond Butter, Cashew Butter, raw nuts of all sorts and just about every vegetable you can imagine. There was not a green leaf left behind!

Then we went online and ordered some of the things not available at Whole Foods.

I was determined to grow my own fresh wheatgrass and forget about the frozen cubes I had previously used. Besides, it was a lot cheaper to grow some of the greens myself. I went online and ordered organic wheatgrass seeds from the Sproutman, the growing cabinets and trays from wheatgrasskits. com and Azomite from Amazon. When a few days later several huge boxes arrived, I almost had a nervous breakdown. The boxes sat on our kitchen floor for at least a couple of weeks, until one day I felt up to the challenge. I opened each box and had another nervous breakdown. There were screws and nails and round things and lights and wires everywhere. The directions came on a sheet the size of a piece of toilet paper. I was about to feel terribly sorry for myself but knew that that wouldn't get the damn thing built. As I sat there with my glass of coconut water in a crystal white wine glass, not getting the slightest buzz, I could hear my dad's voice in my mind:

"Come on Tschilukker, just look at everything and lay it out in an organized fashion. Think and visualize how it will look when it's done. I raised you as my boy, remember, you can do this!" Dad's voice was right.

I took another big gulp of coconut water and went at it. Two and a half hours later it was done. I rolled it into the dining room which has the most natural sun light. Everything was plugged in and all the lights worked. I felt on top of the world and couldn't wait to show Frank. Frank is impressed when I wear matching socks – the fact that I put this thing together totally blew his skirt up!

Eight days later, I cut our own grass and told Randy to cut his deliveries down to Sunflower and Sweet Pea Sprouts.

As we continued on our raw food journey, Frank became thinner and thinner. This concerned us greatly but whenever we voiced our concerns, we were told the following:

"Do not worry about losing weight. The body knows exactly what it must do to heal and with the raw food you are allowing it to do so. You will completely rebuild the body, from the guts on out. It's like buying a fixer upper – you don't just slap a coat of paint on the walls and put new carpets in. You gut it, rip out the old and moldy parts so that you can build it back up the right way." This made a lot of sense and we kept raw.

Tom Tam, in the meantime, kept telling us: "DON'T EAT LIKE COW. EAT COW!" This was somewhat discerning because we trusted Tom implicitly and credited Frank's tremendous healing progress in large part to him. But, we weren't going to falter.

In the meantime, we found yet another gem; Moira Kiley. Moira owns the Hands On Healing Center in Beverly and is a licensed massage therapist, specializing in TuiNa. Both Frank and I see her every other week, usually the week we don't see Tom Tam. TuiNa is the physical part of Tong Ren where blockages along the spine are worked on and loosened.

Staying raw became more and more challenging. Preparing a meal for Sunday evening sometimes meant that I had to start it on Monday morning. Between soaking and sprouting and dehydrating, it could take days to make a more substantial meal. Thank God for Robert's Organic Café in Beverly. We also often visited Alissa Cohen's raw food restaurant in the North End, Grezzo, which Alissa unfortunately eventually closed.

Alissa's food was so delicious that Frank and I signed up to take her four day workshop from May 29 – June 1st, 2009. After completion, we were raw food chefs, teachers and instructors. By now, Frank was down to 152 pounds and now we were terrified.

Marie-Lou, in the meantime, had left for India, setting up house in Kulu where their teacher resides, while Paul was concluding their life here in Massachusetts. I missed her terribly.

# BYE BYE NUTS, HELLO WARM VEGGIES!

A few weeks later, Cecilia called to see how we were doing. I told her that Frank was down to 147 pounds and that we were really scared.

"How about Michael and I come visit you for a few days?" she offered immediately.

"Are you serious? That would be so great" I replied, sighing in relief as a whole lot of help was coming our way.

I went out of my way to impress Cecilia with what I had learned. I must have had eight different dishes on the table, all raw, all vegan, all mostly nut based. I could tell by her first reaction to Frank that she was concerned and after complimenting me on my dinner, she gently said:

"JouJou, this diet is no longer working for Frank. I can tell that his spleen is overworked because his skin looks awful and his lethargy is telling. Besides, due to his enormous stress level, his adrenals aren't functioning well, either. There is too much fat in this food which makes it hard for his body to absorb. May I help you and introduce some steamed and warm foods over the next few days so we can determine whether it is beneficial for him?"

She could have slaughtered a goat on my kitchen table and I would have been fine with it. I was at my wits' end and needed her help more than I could say.

In one week, everything changed for me (again!). Her intuition was dead on and within two days, Franks' color came back, he felt more energetic and he gained a couple of pounds! Angel Number Four and I spent hours in the kitchen, she teaching, me learning and writing almost as fast as she could talk. We made baked root vegetables in a garlic aioli and Frank, after not having had anything warm in over 5 months, felt like he died and went to heaven. The next day we made Quinoa and Millet for breakfast, adding some Macca and Mesquite. I discovered Kukicha Tea with Eden Rice & Soy and I go through a case in a month. We flash sautéed vegetables and made soups for hours on end. We marinated and dehydrated Shiitake and Portobello mushrooms and flavored many things with their tasty and meat like texture. We made delicious desserts using Vanilla flavored Oat Milk, mixed with Kuzu and sweetened with Kal Stevia with Luo Han. It was still all vegan, only a hell of a lot more exciting and at least for us, more nourishing. Cecilia asked me to show her all of my favorite recipes and then she showed me how to make just about all of them in a healthy, vegan way.

Cecilia also told us about another enzyme – Advanced Formula. This was a huge gift since Frank was sick and tired of swallowing fifteen enzymes with each meal. With Advanced Formula you take one. There are different ones for different times:

1 FlorEnz when he first gets up in the morning.
1 DigestEnz with each meal.
1 CarbohydrEnz with a meal rich in carbohydrates
1 LipidEnz if he ever eats a very heavy meal
1 InflammEnz only if there is some kind of inflammation in his body.

# ISRAEL

---

### July 2009

Dealing with cancer is exhausting on every level. We kept fueling ourselves with prayer and healthy nutrition. One thing we wanted to do was to get to know God a little better... We were both reading the bible and decided to see where Jesus lived for ourselves. We had such a need for life at this point that no financial concerns could stop us.

Nearly laughing ourselves off the poor camel

In front of St. Peter's Statue

# RED ROCK RIDE

October 2009

By now, Frank was doing incredibly well on his new diet, weighing a healthy 170 pounds. He felt energetic and feisty and needed an "outlet". I went online and looked for something fun to do. Being a cowgirl at heart, I immediately gravitated towards the Wild West. I found the Red Rock Ride and Frank was just as excited as I was to jump in the saddle. We spent an amazing few days in the most breathtaking scenery imaginable.

Cowboy Frank

Overlooking the Grand Canyon

# HAPPY BIRTHDAY
# TO ME!

---

July 15th, 2010

Frank, the ever more energetically charged hubby, decided to surprise me with a weekend getaway to Nova Scotia. Neither one of us had ever been and it sounded like fun. We had a blast.

# Juliette Guidara

Celebrating my Birthday in Nova Scotia

# AFRICA

---

October 2010

Frank had been telling me about his trip to Africa for years. Understanding and appreciating my love for animals, and as a huge Thank You for helping him get through a couple of tough years, he wanted to show me first hand. It was amazing.

Tanzania. White men truly can't jump!

Well fed lions.  We almost drove over them!

Since we had to fly back home via Europe, we stopped in Switzerland for a few days and went hiking with Mom and Dad.

Sitting by the Aletsch Glacier in Switzerland with mom and dad

# ANOTHER TONG REN MIRACLE

## December 2010

A few days ago I received a frantic call from Roberta Lerman, an "old" hypnotherapy client of mine. She told me that she lost her eyesight in one eye in just a few short days and was worried sick that she might lose her sight in the other eye as well. I immediately offered to record an anti-anxiety session for her, but begged her to let me do some Tong Ren for her as well. In addition, I firmly suggested that she go see Tom Tam. This is the email I received from Roberta a few weeks later.

"Approximately a little over four weeks ago, I woke up with what felt like a smudge covering my eye. I kept trying to wipe it away. My optometrist thought it was the beginnings of an early cataract. He suggested I see an ophthalmologist. However within three days I had completely lost my sight in my left eye. I ended up at the emergency room at Mass Eye and Ear, where after a battery of tests, including an MRI, the diagnosis was that I had Ischemic Optical Neuropathy, which in layman's terms is calcium deposits along my optical nerve choked off the blood flow somewhere along the wire that runs from the brain to my eye, wiping out my sight. I was told I would not get my sight back.

My husband suggested I call Juliette to ask her to make me a CD to help with my stress and anxiety. Juliette through hypnotherapy had been instrumental in my success in quitting a three pack a day cigarette habit five years ago. A fact my husband tells people is miraculous! When I explained to Juliette what was going on with me, she suggested I see Tom Tam, an acupuncturist who also had developed a procedure called Tong Ren.

When Juliette first explained Tong Ren to me, I thought it was beyond silly and way too new age for me. How could someone on a model of a human figure do anything to help me get my sight back? Juliette kept urging me to keep an open mind, suggesting I go and see Tom Tam. I also scheduled some Tong Ren sessions with Juliette to begin a few days after my appointment with Tom Tam.

Desperate at this point to try anything that would help my eye sight, I went to see Tom Tam. After I explained what was wrong with me and what the doctor's prognosis was, I went through my first Tong Ren (tapping session) and an acupuncture session. During and after, all I could think was "this is so nuts". The Tong Ren was relaxing as was the acupuncture, but, I felt different. Nothing had changed. On the drive home, I remember being upset, thinking I was going to remain blind in this eye and maybe it would happen in the other.

When I woke the next day, I turned to look at my husband and realized I could see him. I put my hand over my good eye just to be sure and was absolutely shocked. I could see, not perfectly but the improvement was about 80%. I couldn't believe it! I woke my husband Steve who was just as amazed. I kept closing my good eye every ten minutes or so just to be sure.

Within a few days of this miracle, I experienced my first Tong Ren (tapping) session with Juliette. All I can say is after each session I have had, I have felt relaxed and energized, calm, I felt good inside and out. My eye sight kept improving to the point that it is back to where it was originally.

Going back to Mass Eye to get the results of the MRI and hear what they had to say was an interesting experience. The doctors were flabbergasted to say the least when I told them I could see. They re-ran the series of eye tests, becoming more and more dumbfounded as they realized I could in fact see. My doctor said he couldn't believe it. He had never seen anything like it. He looked at me and said "I don't know what to say". From the last tests and the MRI, he was sure his diagnosis was correct.

I told him about the acupuncture and the Tong Ren. He said "there is a lot to be said for Eastern medicine, I can't discount it. You should not be able to see out of your left eye."

What I know for sure; a few weeks ago I was completely blind in my left eye.

What I know for sure: After a couple of sessions of acupuncture and a few session of Tong Ren my eye sight is back to normal.

My advice-Keep an open mind. You might just be surprised!

Roberta Lerman

# ANOTHER CA19-9 >1

January 27th, 2011

This was Frank's fifth blood test to determine his CA19-9. Due to the statistics, I was pretty worried about it. We were going into Frank's third year and this was an important one. I was laying on Moira Kiley's massage table when my phone rang.

"Honey, breathe, relax but jump up and down", Frank's happy voice said. "My CA19-9 once again is less than one!"

Moira and I screamed for joy, high-fived each other and smiled like cats in a cream tub.

# A CRUISE TO CELEBRATE

February 27th – March 12th, 2011

To celebrate God and life and love, we decided to join my mom and dad on a cruise to the Caribbean. None of us had ever been on a cruise and we were so looking forward to spending time together. This was going to be great; nobody had to cook or shop or clean up. All we did was talk, relax, play cards, laugh, read, eat and dance! Frank, who initially wasn't thrilled with a "boring" vacation, radiated with health and vitality afterwards!

Before mom and dad went back to Switzerland, Will invited us to visit his restaurant, Eleven Madison Park in New York City, where he and Daniel Humm spoiled us rotten!

Frank at Devil's Bay, Virgin Gorda, (Yummy!)

Will, Mom, Dad, me, Frank and Daniel Humm.
At Eleven Madison Park, March 2011.

# VISIT FROM THE PHAL'S

April 16th -18th, 2011

Charles and Sharon Phal, whom we'd befriended at Hippocrates, came for a visit. I had told them all about Tong Ren and they were curious. I spent several hours showing Sharon how to tap for Charles, who had stage 4 kidney / liver cancer, and to this day he is doing fantastically well. *[Tong Ren is not the only treatment Charles received]*.

# BIG SCARE, BIG RELIEF

August 16<sup>th</sup>, 2011

Frank came home early today – never a good sign. He was shaking and had a fever. He immediately called Dr. Abramson who prescribed some antibiotics, asking him to come in for an appointment. He couldn't find anything wrong.

August 22<sup>nd</sup>, 2011

Frank came home early again, this time with severe stomach pains and suffering from diarrhea. We thought that he might have pulled a stomach muscle during our nine mile walk on Sunday. But, the pain persisted and the next day, he called Dr. Ferrone. She scheduled a CT scan for the evening of the 24th.

Frank was concerned that the pain might suggest that the cancer was back, and even though I was scared, I was able to convince both of us that cancer wouldn't just show up with debilitating pain overnight.

Frank's initial protocol asked for scans every three months post surgery. We never did one. It was time to face the music.

August 25th, 2011

We were on pins and needles. On one hand, I knew that cancer didn't stand a chance in Frank's body after everything we had done. One the other hand, cancer does not always obey. I was ready for another restless night.

August 26th, 2011

We had a 7:00 a.m. appointment with Dr. Ferrone. It was a long night and as I walked out the door into the garage, my phone told me that I had a text message from Cristina from the evening before: "CTs look good! C u tomorrow." I could not believe that I missed that text. I jumped into the car and told Frank:

"CT scans are perfect honey!"

"How do you know that?!" he asked.

I promptly shoved my phone under his nose out of which came the biggest sigh of relief.

As promised, the scans were clear from head to toe with the exception of one tiny little spot near the lung, which Cristina was not at all worried about.

Turns out that my dearly beloved husband had been sneaking coffee at work and the acidity from that caused the pain! I was really glad though, because it forced us to have a scan and now we know that Frank's insides are healthy and clean. Thank God!

Dr. Ferrone also mentioned to us that she was trying to get funding for a new pancreatic cancer patient protocol which would involve radiation, surgery and an immune system enhancing drug, instead of Chemo. I was stunned. I promised her immediately that I would donate a certain percentage from the sales of this book to it.

# MEETING WITH
# DR. GUNDRY

November 1st, 2011

Our angel Cecilia had been begging us to go see a doctor friend of hers, Dr. Steven Gundry. From his website, www.drgundry.com:

"Dr. Gundry has gone on to be internationally recognized as an inventor, researcher and one of "America's Top Doctors." Dr. Gundry's accomplishments in areas like robotic assisted heart surgery, congenital heart surgery, heart transplantation, cardioplegia catheters, minimally invasive valve surgery, mechanical support devices for the failing heart and reanimation of "dead" hearts have contributed greatly to advancements in cardiac care. He's been the Head of the Division of Cardiothoracic Surgery, Medical Director of Adult and Pediatric Cardiac Surgical ICU's, and Program Director of the Cardiothoracic Residency Program at Loma Linda University School of Medicine while continuing his numerous research projects. He is also a founding board member of the Society of Minimally Invasive Cardiac Surgery. Dr. Gundry has written more than 200 articles and books about cardiac surgery, and the nutritional reversal of heart disease, high cholesterol, diabetes and hypertension.

Today Dr. Gundry is the Director of The International Heart and Lung Institute in Palm Springs, California, and the Founder/Director of The Center for Restorative Medicine in Palm Springs and Santa Barbara. But he is destined to be known by everyday people outside his field as the author of the life-changing book *Dr. Gundry's Diet Evolution: Turn Off the Genes That Are Killing You – and Your Waistline – and Drop the Weight for Good*. Quite a mouthful, it is fast becoming the new Bible for smart eating…and its secrets extend far beyond what people believe is the obvious."

Since listening to this angel has paid off big time so far, we happily agreed to an appointment.  Back in September, Dr. Gundry's office had sent us clear instructions for blood draws, which we then sent to his lab.

We met Cecilia for lunch in some vegan restaurant in Palm Springs before heading off to our appointment.  Following her in our rental, I mumbled:

"I hope this is not going to be a waste of time, Frank."

"Me, too"

At that point, we had no idea who this Dr. Gundry was and what he was all about.

Without going into the details of our meeting, let me just say that we never knew tests like his existed.  In our one hour meeting, Dr. Gundry clearly stated why we were going to suffer from certain guaranteed ailments, and how to completely eliminate their threat with vitamins and/or supplements.  Instead of selling us his own brand, he suggested that we go to Costco or Vitacost.com.

We were absolutely amazed and beyond impressed.  Never would we have believed what Dr. Gundry could see in our blood.  So now, with his and

Cecilia's help, our daily intake of vitamins and supplements has changed. It is an insane amount of pills, but they are working beautifully for us! And as always, we continue to work out just about every day, lifting weights, riding the bike, yoga or turning ourselves into sweat hogs on the elliptical.

# DREAM TRIP TO ARGENTINA

---

March 11ᵗʰ – March 23ʳᵈ, 2012

Frank always wanted to visit the Napa Valley of Argentina, Mendoza. This vacation had it all – the most generous, warm hospitality of the Catena Family at La Vendimia, an adventures trip up into the Andes, and a few culture filled days in Buenos Aires. The day I get the first copy of my book in the mail, we will open our first bottle Catena Malbec Argentino, my favorite.

Frank proudly stated that we'd be staying at the "Hotel of a Million Stars" high up in the Andes. I, of course, searched for hours to try to find it online, with no success. After riding for about 6 – 7 hours, we finally came across a patch of dirt that was not covered in rocks and our gaucho guide, who looked exactly like John Wayne, proudly declared: "Welcome to the Hotel of a Million Stars!" and threw a couple of tents at us. Perfect!

In Buenos Aires, we had arranged for a four hour private tango lesson. Ten minutes into it, our very serious teacher took Frank aside and instructed him to gaze at me with anger and passion while leading me (in my socks) around the floor. Frank tried, but his effort resulted in me having a total and utter laughing fit. Those aren't pretty, by the way. There were tears

277

streaming down my face, along with snot and I was doubled over in hysterics making sounds that would scare a wild boar. On top of that, they last for quite a while. While Frank, somewhat amused, was patiently waiting for the fit to pass, our teacher was outraged and left! He did come back after about fifteen minutes and of course, ended up falling in love with us. He showed Frank all around the place while I picked splinters out of my feet.

Picking grapes (ok, eating them) at one of Catena's famous vineyards.

The luxurious "Hotel of a Million Stars!"

# READING ABOUT EATING

Over the past few years, both Frank and I read tons of books which were life changing. The ones that truly stand out are "The China Study" by T. Colin Campbell, PhD & Thomas M. Campbell II. It is without a doubt the most comprehensive book on nutrition we have found to date. It is based on a forty year study that proves how consuming animal proteins affect our health. It also addresses the power of the FDA, the Pharmaceutical Companies, the Dairy Industry and the Cattlemen Association, among many others.

"Eating Animals" by Jonathan Safran Foer was the most difficult book for me to read. I got through it sobbing and waking up from nightmares. In it Jonathan talks about how our animals are raised and slaughtered for human consumption. He also talks about the horrendous effects the meat and dairy industry have on the environment. If you love animals and care about the environment, this one's for you.

Frank also liked "The Omnivores Dilemma" by Michael Pollan, but after having read more than my share of books about animals' suffering, I couldn't stomach another. I took Frank's word for it.

The Hippocrates Health Institute sells a documentary called "Eating". We found it life changing.

# TODAY

May 2012

Frank and I are feeling better than ever before. His weight is stable at 170 pounds and he looks incredible! Frank still gets up every morning to make himself two ounces of wheatgrass juice followed by a 16 ounce glass of green juice. In addition, he is enjoying raw, homemade energy bars. In the winter, he will switch to soups again. Leeks, red onion, Miso, Spinach and Coconut oil, blended with hot water, Bragg's, vegan bouillon and herbs, as well as lots of greens; either Kale or Spinach. For lunch he enjoys salads and veggies, and instead of coming home to a martini, he comes home to more wheatgrass and another green juice. Dinners consist of either huge salads or Shirataki pasta with lots of garlic and greens and once in a while, some wild caught seafood. When in season, we pig out on artichokes. His daily allotment of red wine is six ounces which he enjoys tremendously. Goat and sheep cheeses frequently visit as desserts, along with the six ounces of wine. Those we enjoy with flax seed crackers or pumpkin seed crackers. It is a restricted way of eating and you might wonder if it's worth it. The answer is: Absolutely!

The reason we stay away from American Cow's milk is because all proteins are long chains of amino acids. Beta casein (the protein in cow's milk) is a chain 229 amino acid in length. Cows who produce this protein in their milk with a proline at number 67 are called A2 cows, and are the older breeds of cows (i.e. Jerseys, Asian, African, European cows). But some 5,000 years ago, a mutation occurred in this proline amino acid, converting it to histidine. Cows that have this mutated beta casein (American cows) are called A1 cows, and include breeds like Holstein. Proline has a strong bond to a small protein called BCM7, which helps keep it from getting into the milk, so that essentially no BCM7 is found in the urine, blood or GI tract of old-fashioned A2 cows. On the other hand, histidine, the mutated protein (from American cows) only weakly holds on to BCM7, so it is liberated in the GI tract of animals and humans who drink A1 cows milk. BCM7 has been shown to cause neurological impairment in animals and people exposed to it, especially autistic and schizophrenic changes. BCM7 interferes with the immune response, and injecting BCM7 in animal models has been shown to provoke type 1 diabetes. Dr. Woodford's book presents research showing a direct correlation between a population's exposure to A1 cow's milk and incidence of autoimmune disease, heart disease, type 1 diabetes, autism and schizophrenia. (resource: Dr. Thomas Cowan).

People often ask me how I was able to cope with this ordeal. My answer is always the same; most days, thanks to my faith, I felt strong and able to deal. Other days; not so much. I remember two specific incidents that totally knocked me down.

One night, a couple of years ago, Frank was out of town and I was watching "House", one of my favorite TV Shows. In this particular episode, Dr. Wilson pulled the life support on his girlfriend. It was about 10 pm and I totally lost it. *Oh God, what if I'm ever confronted with a situation like this?*

I once again reached out to Micki, who ended up talking to me for over two hours, while we both gulped several glasses of wine.

Another bad day was September 14ᵗʰ, 2009 when Patrick Swayze passed away. My heart broke for him and his wife Lisa. I had a pretty good idea of what they both had been through.

During those times, there is a little voice in the back of my head that keeps reminding me that we might face the same fate one day. I now tell that voice to go find another home.

Our journey of teaching and learning will never stop. We will continue to read and study and keep an open mind. Adversity is a terrible thing to waste and we are dedicated to a willingness to change and adapt.

I continue to meditate and get a tremendous amount of faith and strength from it. When I pray, I grow stronger in my faith and trust in God. I now calmly trust God that whatever happens, it will be ok. My fear of death has greatly diminished as I no longer look at the physical as a representation of being. As a matter of fact, I think of people as light bulbs; some shine a little brighter than others, but we all try to stand out and hold on to our individual uniqueness. And while the process of dying scares me, death itself is but another door to walk through, into the light, into the essence of what we truly are. I don't mind losing my mistaken identity as a light bulb when I know I will be a part of the sun, connected once again with my creator and all of creation.

In closing, I'd like to share my method of meditating and praying with you.

In the past, whenever I "tried" to meditate, I attempted to quiet my mind. Then I'd get frustrated when it didn't work. I don't think it ever worked!

Now when I meditate, I let the mind do its thing while I concentrate on what's "behind" my mind. For me it's a sensation of beaming a light channel from my spine right through the top of my head. There's a slight lengthening sensation and sometimes it feels as if the top of my head gives way. The stronger the beam of light, the less "top of the head" and the less I care what my mind is doing. It can do its thing while I do mine since I am no longer identifying with it. I feel the connection of the earth below and heaven above.

I then imagine myself walking down a beautiful hallway. Lush carpet under my feet, the windows open with white curtains blowing in the wind. Amazing pictures of us and our family and friends are on the walls, perfectly displayed. At the end of the hallway is an elevator. I push the down button, and the elevator takes me gently down, down, down. When the doors open, I find myself in paradise! There's a beautiful black Frisian (a horse, not a man) waiting for me. I nuzzle him and then jump on top of him for an amazing ride through heaven. The horse knows exactly where I want to go and takes me straight to Jesus. Sometimes he is in a meadow, other times underneath a big tree. When I get there, I sometimes massage his shoulders or his feet, other times I just snuggle up. Then, I listen.

# SUMMARY

---

- We should have listened to Frank's body years ago. He had been suffering from all kinds of stomach issues: GERD, Acid Reflux, Heartburn, Gas, etc. He was popping Gaviscon like they were candy.

Once we learned about the importance that the food intake sequence has, all of his symptoms went away.

  o We always eat fruit on an empty stomach, by itself.

  o We never drink water or anything cold with a meal to allow the gastric juices do their job without dilution.

  o We begin meals with a salad, followed by veggies, followed by "whatever".

  o The Reason? It takes your stomach approximately 10 – 20 minutes to digest fruit. About 30 minutes to digest veggies, about 1 hour to digest most carbohydrates and up to 2 hours to digest animal protein. If you start with a steak, then have the veggies followed by a salad, the veggies cannot pass through and neither can the salad. They sit on top of the protein and begin to ferment and create gas resulting in an upset stomach.

- We found out that it is crucial to seek out the best, most qualified doctor / surgeon for whatever ailment or disease we are dealing with.

- When Frank was initially diagnosed, we were scared to death. We had no idea what to do or where to turn to. It was great to learn about all the various resources that are available; traditional and alternative / complementary like acupuncture, tui na massage and ChiGong.

- Of course, we always find out where a Tom Tam Tong Ren Guinea Pig Class is: http://www.tomtam.com/guinea-pig-class-directory or a Tong Ren Conference Call: http://www.tomtam.com/tong-ren-conference-call

- Frank loved listening to the hypnotherapy CDs I made for him. Immune System Strengthening, Pre-Surgery and Post –Surgery. If you are interested, you can order CDs from my website: JulietteGuidara. com or you can send me an email at Juliette@CenterOfThought.com

- To deal with the Chemo, Frank found the organic seaweed baths from Benedetta highly detoxifying. He also took steam showers infused with Eucalyptus, Red Thyme, Rosewood and White Camphor.

- We learned about the cancer fighting compounds in Wheatgrass and the immune system strengthening properties of green juices and will never go without them.

  o Juicer: We use a Green Power Twin Gear which works great for Wheatgrass, Green Juices and all other juices. We got ours from www.my-greenpower-juicer.com

o Wheatgrass: You can buy it fresh at Whole Foods or other organic supermarkets. Or, you can perhaps find a local distributor. You can also grow your own! It's pretty easy and not too time consuming.

- Wheatgrass Seeds we get from: www.sproutman.com

- Wheatgrass growing kit we got from: www.wheatgrasskits.com

o Green Juice: organic cucumber, celery, sunflower sprouts and sweet pea sprouts. Again, you should be able to find those in your local health food store or via local supplier. If not, you can grow them yourself.

• Frank did really well with the supplements we took home from Hippocrates. We continue with them today. www.hippocratesinst.org

• We learned that fresh coconut water (from virgin / baby green or white coconuts) has tremendous health benefits, including pancreatic enzymes. All you need is a meat cleaver. This video explains it beautifully: http://www.youtube.com/watch?v=1HqVMYCr8MU

• Exercise and fresh air are a huge part of our lives.

• Along with any food intake, Frank takes Advanced Formula digestive enzymes.

# MY HIPPOCRATES NOTES

- Everyone carries his personal doctor inside; the Immune System. When the Immune System has to deal with the constant bombardment of animal protein (meat and dairy), yeast, sugar and alcohol, it is already way too overwhelmed to deal with dis-ease.

- The rate of blood cell formation varies depending on the individual, but a typical production might average 200,000,000,000 red cells per day, 10,000,000,000 white cells per day, and 400,000,000,000 platelets per day. Approximately 1% of those are cancerous. A healthy Immune System immediately recognizes the threat and destroys it.

- Many of us focus on food as the main theme of our existence since we have unhappy and unfulfilling lives. The question most asked is, "How can I forego this pleasurable aspect of life?" The answer is clear: "Once you have a life worth living, you do not required food to take the place of fulfillment."

- Genesis 1:29 The God said, "I give you every seed bearing plant on the face of the whole earth and every tree that has fruit with seed in it. They will be yours for food.

- Genesis 1:30 "And to all the beasts of the earth and all the birds of the air and all the creatures that move on the ground, everything that has the breath of life in it, I give every green plant for food."

- 97% of North America's Soy Crop has been genetically modified.

- One hour of using a cell, mobile or wireless phone per day can increase the risk of brain tumors by 100%.

- Animal fat / cholesterol is directly linked to every major disease known to man: cancer, heart disease, diabetes, etc.

- In North America, half of those 55 years of age and younger will contract some sort of cancer.

- In adult population, 50% of 40-year old men cannot perform sexually and the median age for menopause has dropped by 10 years in the last 30 years due to animal protein consumption.

- The FDA's recommends "3-glasses of milk a day". 3 glasses of milk contain the same amount of cholesterol found in 53 slices of bacon!

- One cubic centimeter of cow's milk is allowed to contain up to 750,000 pus cells and up to 20,000 live bacteria!

- Sugar is sugar – avoid when Immune System is compromised (i.e. dealing with cancer). For 2 years, avoid all fruits and all natural sweeteners such as honey, agave, etc. The only safe sweetener is Stevia.

- Because it kills life, salt is considered by many to be a great food preservative, as it prevents spoilage for months to years on end. AVOID ALL SALTS. Use Nama Shoyu or Bragg's Amino Acids.

- The very best source of minerals is in plant foods.

- Coffee is acid-forming in the body rather than alkalizing, and decaf coffee is even more acidic than regular.

- Cancer cells cannot live in an alkaline environment (ph of 7.3+) PH = Potential Hydrogen. They feed on sugar and yeast.

- Anne Wigmore's initial protocol:

  o 1. Sprouts. When sprouting, wait until the sprout has an "offspring" this puts the sprout into the Mother position, capable of producing 100s more "offspring". A sprout is numerously more nutritious than any seed. 10x more than any vegetable. Wheatgrass is 30x more nutritious than any vegetable.

  o 2. Sea Vegetables – most nutritious in the ocean.

  o 3. Fresh Water algae – most nutritious in Fresh Water. (Blue, Blue/Green).

The brain is the epicenter of our system.  It has 8.5 x more cells than the rest of our body.  85 Trillion cells are in the brain.  10 Trillion in the rest of body.

The heart is like a beautiful sailboat.  The mind is the rudder.  Today's life is like being in the ocean with the rudder and no boat, wondering why we're sinking.

You are what you absorb:  The small intestine is 22 feet long and 90% of all absorption takes place there.

# THE THREE REASONS THIS PROGRAM HEALS / WORKS:

**1.ALL LIFE COMES FROM THE SUN** (Sprouts)
Consuming food with the most sunlight in it (fresh, organic, raw, living foods) will heal and build my body at maximum levels.

**2.CONSUMING PRE DIGESTED FOODS** (juice, sprouts and algae's) will give my body ultimate nutrition without utilizing massive energy for digestion which can go for vitality and healing.

**3.ENZYME RICH FOODS** (raw, organic, vegan, living foods) will increase the electromagnetic frequency in and around my cells, preventing free radical damage - the cause of all premature aging and disease.

- Don't wear nylon clothing – they produce estrogen in the body!

- Chia and Hemp Seeds are the most fabulous fats.

- No. 1 Grains: Millet, Buckwheat, Teff, Amaranth, Quinoa. These grains give you tons of energy. Meat has 19% protein, these have 25% protein.

- Beans: for energy.  ALL EXCEPT BLACK BEANS AND SOY BEANS, they are too hibernated and their molecular structure has been changed.  If using Black Beans or Soy Beans, make sure they are organic and GMO free.

- Chickpeas give you the most energy.

- Adzuki beans are terrific for the lungs, bladder and kidneys.

- Mung beans for minerals (the long, white Chinese sprouts).  They are the easiest to digest.  Water is number one, mung bean sprouts number two, plus they are loaded with Zinc.

- Dandelions clean the liver and blood.

- Nettles melt fat.

- Cleaning Products:  Shackley, Amway, 7th Generation.

- Fenugreek encodes gastro intestinal function (pancreatic function and blood sugar)

- STANDARD BELIEF IS: 40% Protein, 50% carbs, 20% fat.

- TRUE HEALTHY LIVING: 5% Protein, 90% carbs, 5% fat.

- 1 egg has 230 mg cholesterol and can only be digested by a fox.  It turns into "rubber" in the human stomach.

- Free Radical:  Imagine a red blood cell with two electric charges.  When a toxic substance (meat, dairy, alcohol) is introduced, the "meat" of the red blood cells is destroyed, leaving the two electric charges to run rampant; going after other electrics and forming gangs. Those are free radicals.

- Wear only organic cotton clothing. ¼ of all pesticide used today is on cotton.

- Nylon promotes estrogen which releases electrics which release free radicals which can cause cancer.

- The brain is the only organ in the body functioning at 3 – 5%

- Sleeping less than 6.5 hours per night increases the risk of cancer 3 – 4 times.

- The sun is the number 1 Immune System booster.

- Everything you've ever learned, experienced and known/perceived is your universe. With each disappointment, that universe gets smaller and smaller. To fix that, we have to face what we fear the most and make it bigger!

- Don't reduce your life and identify with who you are to a disease (I'm the guy with pancreatic cancer).

- With each problem you expect, anticipate and count on, your world becomes smaller.

- Find a REAL reason to live for yourself, not because somebody else needs you.

- Live your Passion, that's how you heal yourself.

- o Moses, 40 years in the desert walking

- o Jesus, forgiving the man who stabbed him while on the cross

- o Ghandi; used the above messages to create peace

- o Mandela

- o King

- o ALWAYS ACT AND BEHAVE AS THOUGH GOD IS WATCHING YOU.

- FILL YOURSELF WITH LOVE AND THERE IS NO ROOM FOR ILLNESS.

- WHEN YOU MOVE TO A PLACE OF COMPLETE PASSION, YOU WILL BE AT A PLACE OF UNWAIVERING COMMITMENT (because it turns you on).

- To digest dairy, you have to steel calcium from your bones.

- Cholesterol is a bigger killer than all wars put together.

- Cholesterol count needs to be under 150.

- Breast cancer: on a plant based diet, there is a 0% chance of recurrence. Animal based diet 38% chance of recurrence.

- Beef without subsidies would be $90 per pound.

- The doctors of the future will know how to prescribe food, exercise and nutrition.

- It takes 13 pounds of grain to grow 1 pound of beef.

- It takes 5 pounds of feed to grow 1 pound of salmon.

- The appetite for beef is the major factor for global warming.

- In an acidic body, the blood cells clump together and cannot enter the blood stream.

- Dry skin is a result of low lipids.

- At 30 years old, you get half the cellular turn-over as an 18 year old.

- Commercial soaps thicken the skin and are acidic.

- The activity of life is enzyme-activity.

- Eating cooked foods causes a pathogenic response called leukocytosis which is white blood cells attacking the cooked food like they would a foreign substance.

- Germination: it removes certain metabolic inhibitors which exist to protect the seed from bacteria and preserve it in its dormant state.

- A blender makes fruits or vegetables appear liquefied compared to a juicer which extracts only the juice.

- Wheatgrass: one of the riches sources of Vitamins A, C and E contains all the known mineral elements and exceptionally high in B Vitamins.

Chlorophyll creates an unfavorable environment for bacteria growth and eliminates toxins.

- Steam baths clean the water organs (lungs, kidneys, bladder).

- Sauna cleans fat organs (liver, gallbladder).

- A whirlpool benefits nerve tissue and bones.

- Alcohol: the body utilizes all forms of alcohol as pure sugar.

- Eating starches and proteins together create a sulfur compound creating gas.

- Human body regenerates within a 7 year period.

- Brain works 24 hours whereas the body takes a break, hence the brain needs 8 ½ times more energy.

- Stress causes body to generate cholesterol.

- Less food, longer life.

- More people die today from too much food, not starvation.

- Fasting can add many years to your life.

- We are the first experimental generation without exercise.

- High estrogen levels increase chance of cancer.

- A Baby's crawling develops its mind.

- 100% raw diet is ideal.

- 80:20 = 20% of food consumed is not raw.

- 70:30 the immune system's ability to fight disease is lowered by 17.6%

- Anything beyond 70:30 weakens it by 48%.

- Blue green algae are chlorophyll rich, single cell life form; supplies complete protein and strengthen the red blood cells.

- Our intestinal organs digest food and emotions.

- As you think you are.

- Fructose is refined from corn starch and is converted into fatty acids when consumed and not used (burned).

- Raw Honey is a good antioxidant; the darker, the better and it may help with allergies, but is still predominantly sugar.

- Blue green algae capture free radicals.

# FOOD RELATED

- Tomatoes are a fruit. Do not combine with vegetables. Combine tomatoes with avocadoes, onion and garlic.

- 3 Types of fruit: Acidic, sub-acidic and sweet. Never mix and always eat melons alone, by themselves, on an empty stomach.

- Add blended zucchini and/or squash to salad dressings for texture and more substance.

- Only eat orange and red bell peppers (not under ripe green ones) and lots of radishes. They fight cancer.

- Snacks: "Living Nutz". They are already soaked and dehydrated.

- When eating dehydrated foods, drink a lot of water. The body will take it one way or another.

- Best oils to use: Hemp Oil, Flax oil, Extra Virgin Cold Pressed Olive Oil, Sesame Oil.

- In cheese: avoid "casein" ingredient at all cost. Only buy vegan cheeses and sparingly.

- Tempeh – only soy product to use and sparingly. Slice, steam and use for a "chicken salad" once a month.

- Manna Bread and Ezekiel Whole Rye and Millet (gluten and yeast free).

- Pizza: Amy's spinach w/ Rice Crust, gluten and dairy free.

- Buckwheat grouts – sprout and serve for breakfast.

- Instead of tomatoes for sauces, use blended red bell peppers.

- Pasta: Andean Dream Quinoa, Kamut, Buckwheat Soba and Spelt.

- Sea Veggies; Nori sheets, Dulse Flakes. Kombu and Aikame for soups. Miso – soy for soups (little).

- Chips: Guiltless Gourmet All Natural Blue Corn

- Cereal: Kamut and Millet Puffs. Never eat with nut milk, use grain milk or Good Karma Organic Rice Milk (or millet milk).

- Flavored Stevia by Sweet Leaf for teas or Pure Stevia Extract by "Kal" powder.

- Avoid all beauty products containing "Sodium Laurel (or Laureth) Sulfate".

- NO Antiperspirants

- NO Fluoride in toothpaste!

To contact Juliette or to schedule consultations, or order CDs, please visit www.JulietteGuidara.com or email: Juliette@CenterOfThought.com

# RESOURCES

Marie-Lou Kuhne-Millerick, Synergy Healing

"Walking out of the Medical Jungle", Tom Tam

"Walking out of the Medical Jungle", Dr. William C. Daly, M.D.

"Walking out of the Medical Jungle", Dr. Shaw Spraque

"Tom Tam Healing System", Tom Tam

"Cancer for Tong Ren", Rick Kuethe

"The Wheatgrass Book", Ann Wigmore

"Hippocrates Health Institute" Handout Materials

"Quantum Healing", Deepak Chopra, MD

"The China Study", T. Colin Campbell, Ph.D. and Thomas M. Campbell II

"Eating Animals" Jonathan Safran Foer

"The Omnivores' Dilemma" Michael Pollan

"Knockout", Suzanne Somers

"Questioning Chemotherapy", Ralph W. Moss, PhD

"The Politics of Cancer Revisited", Samuel Epstein, MD

"Scientific Medicine Stymied", Professor Georges Mathe

"Why We're Still Dying to Know the Truth", Phillip Day

"Tong Ren for Cancer": A New Way to Heal, Part Two by Rick Kuethe

"Scientific American", John Cairns, Professor of Microbiology, Harvard University

"The Australia Study" Graeme Morgan, MD, Robyn Ward, MD, Michael Barton, MD

"Journal of Clinical Oncology", Heine Hansen, MD

"Cancer: Why We're Still Dying to Know the Truth", Phillip Day

From the article "Chemotherapy: Snake-Oil Remedy", Alan C. Nixon

All Natural Scientific Cancer Research Information:

http://www.1cure4cancer.com/controlcancer/information/chemo.htm

# QUOTES BY:

———————

**Mitch Albom,** "Tuesdays with Morrie"

**Louise L. Hay**

**Washington Irving**

**Deepak Chopra, MD:** "Quantum Healing – Exploring the Frontiers of Mind/Body Medicine"

**Ralph W. Moss, PhD:**

**Lucien Israel, MD:**

**Alan C. Nixon, PhD**

**Samuel Epstein, MD**

**Majid Ali, MD**

Phillip Day

Professor Georges Mathe

Richard A. Jaffe, Esq.

Suzanne Somers

Nicolas Gonzales, MD

Albert Braverman, MD / Oncologist

Professor John Cairns

Graeme Morgan, MD

Robyn Ward, MD

Michael Barton, MD

Heine Hansen, MD

Made in the USA
Monee, IL
20 October 2022